SADAT

SADAT

THE MAN WHO CHANGED MID-EAST HISTORY

BY GEORGE SULLIVAN

WALKER AND COMPANY  NEW YORK

TO TIM, FOR HELPING

Library of Congress Cataloging in Publication Data

Sullivan, George, 1927.
  Sadat: the man who changed Mid-East history.

  Includes index.
  Summary. Traces the rise of Anwar el-Sadat from
his peasant origins to the presidency of Egypt.
Nobel Peace Prize winner, and dominant figure in
world politics.
    1. Sadat, Anwar, 1918—   —Juvenile literature.
  2. Egypt—Presidents—Biography—Juvenile litera-
ture. [1. Sadat, Anwar, 1918-   2. Egypt—
Presidents] I. Title.
DT107.85.S84 1981 962'.054'0924 [B] [92] 81-50739
ISBN 0-8027-6434-7   AACR2
ISBN 0-8027-6435-5 (lib. bdg.)

MANY PEOPLE HELPED IN THE PREPARATION OF THIS BOOK. SPECIAL THANKS ARE
DUE MOHAMED HAKKI, MINISTER, PRESS AND INFORMATION BUREAU, EMBASSY OF
THE ARAB REPUBLIC OF EGYPT, FOR HIS INTEREST AND COOPERATION. THE
AUTHOR IS ALSO GRATEFUL TO HARPER & ROW, PUBLISHERS, INC., NEW YORK,
FOR PERMISSION TO REPRINT EXCERPTS FROM *IN SEARCH OF IDENTITY*, BY ANWAR
EL-SADAT; AND TO *THE NEW YORK TIMES* AND *THE NEW YORKER* TO QUOTE
BRIEF PASSAGES.

*First published in the United States of America in 1981 by the Walker Publishing
Company, Inc.*

*Published simultaneously in Canada by John Wiley & Sons Canada Limited, Rexdale,
Ontario*

ISBN: 0-8027-6434-7 (cloth)
*   0-8027-6435-5 (reinforced)*

Library of Congress Catalog Card Number: 81-50739

Printed in the United States of America

Book design by Robert Barto

10 9 8 7 6 5 4 3 2 1

CHAPTER 1

ON A SUN-FILLED AFTERNOON ON the last day of March, 1979, a huge jetliner dipped out of the sky to begin its approach to Cairo International Airport. Aboard was Egyptian President Anwar el-Sadat. He was returning from Washington where, five days before, he had signed a historic peace treaty with Prime Minister Menahem Begin of Israel and United States President Jimmy Carter in ceremonies televised around the world from the North Lawn of the White House. Sadat and his handsome wife, Jihan, occupied a comfortable forward cabin in the aircraft. Behind them the seats were filled with ministers, attendants, secretaries, and armed security guards.

Thousands of Egyptians were waiting at the airport to greet Sadat. A crowd that police later estimated at two million lined the route the president's motorcade would follow from the airport to his residence in Giza, a suburb of Cairo.

The big airplane made a smooth landing. With its engines whining, it pulled slowly off the runway to a taxi strip leading to a roped-off area, where the crowd waited. As the plane drew to a stop, a flower-decorated ramp was wheeled to the front door.

The door slid open. The crowd grew silent in anticipation. Then President Sadat appeared in the doorway. He smiled and waved. The crowd sent up a thunderous cheer.

Sadat was tall, trim, and very brown. He had a well-groomed mustache, gleaming dome, and heavily lidded eyes. He wore a tailored suit and black zippered boots. He appeared tired, as he slowly descended the ramp.

He stood at attention, looking serious, as a band played the national anthem. After inspecting the green-uniformed honor guard, Sadat broke into a smile and began working his way down the long line of several hundred officials—diplomats, Muslim and Christian religious leaders, and legislators—who had come to greet him.

Then he entered a sleek, black, open limousine for the hour-long ride to Giza. With his wife at his side and security men on both running boards, Sadat stood and waved to the cheering multitude.

The crowd that lined the roadway included men and women, old people, and children. There were middle-class couples in suits and dresses. There were boys and girls (the schools had been let out for the occasion) in blue jeans. There were bearded sheikhs. The people sang, danced, and clapped. They played bagpipes, harmonicas, and different kinds of stringed instruments.

Pictures of Sadat were everywhere. His portrait had even been woven into souvenir carpets that were being offered for sale.

Thousands of signs hailed Sadat and the era of peace he had long sought. "Peace is the Cherished Aim of the People," one said. Another sign, in the center of Cairo, proclaimed: "To the Mothers of the War Dead Who Gave Their Lives for Egypt." Another, near Sadat's residence, asked, "Why Peace? What Has War Done For Us?".

All over Cairo papier-mâché white doves of peace and banners hailing Sadat as a "Hero of Peace" could be seen. The city was decorated with triumphal arches of bright cloth. That night the Egyptian capital twinkled with thousands of small, colored lights that festooned every city building from banks to gasoline stations.

Egyptians had good reason to thirst for peace. In four bloody Arab wars against Israel—in 1948, 1956, 1967, and 1973—Egypt, of all the Arab states, had absorbed the heaviest losses. Hopes of peace had been raised many times before. Even now, amid the joy and celebrating, no one was willing to say that "real peace" or "permanent peace" was at hand. But certainly the prospects for peace were brighter now than at any time in more than thirty years. And that was enough to evoke great jubilation.

Sadat credits the Egyptian people with creating the era of peace. He tells visiting journalists to walk through the

The President and Mrs. Sadat in a recent photograph.

(PRESS & INFORMATION BUREAU, EMBASSY OF THE ARAB REPUBLIC OF EGYPT)

streets of Cairo, to go anywhere in Egypt, and ask the people if they want peace. "Ask and see," Sadat says.

While Sadat is quick to salute the "will of the people," many observers give him the bulk of the credit. Not only had he possessed a deep-seated resolve that peace be achieved, he was willing to seize fresh approaches and take both personal and political risks on behalf of the negotiations.

As a result of his efforts, Sadat, in 1981, at the age of sixty-two, was hailed as the "architect of a new Mideast" and ranked as a dominant and often-dazzling figure on the stage of international politics. Yet only ten years before he was being laughed at by world leaders as a clown. And in 1970, when Sadat was Egypt's vice-president, his predecessor as president mocked him as "old Goha," a legendary victim, or "fall guy," in Egyptian folklore. He once said that "Sadat's greatest ambition is to own a big automobile and have the government pay for the gasoline."

Sadat's transformation to heroic leader was only one of a number of changes that have characterized his life. He was born a poor peasant. A peasant, according to the dictionary, is not merely an individual engaged in farm labor. In Egypt, as well as in America, a peasant is regarded as a rude, unsophisticated, and usually uneducated person. While Sadat has never sought to deny his background, indeed, he sometimes revels in it, he has had to overcome the burdens associated with the peasant image.

As a young man, Sadat was a terrorist; his hate was focused on the British and the corrupt Egyptian monarchy. His terrorist activities led to two prison terms.

4

His next role was that of loyal government servant, and it was one that he played for almost two decades.

Nothing that Sadat did in the past comes close to approaching his successful struggle to achieve peace in the Middle East. By breaking the long cycle of killing and hatred that had for so long gripped the area, Anwar el-Sadat has won the enduring gratitude of his people and, indeed, of the entire world.

Egypt is the birthplace of civilization, its history going back to the ancient pharaohs, to a time more than five thousand years ago. Through the centuries, dynasty followed dynasty with scarcely any interruption, compiling a record for government durability that has never been matched. If America and its system of government were to endure to the year 4776, it would merely equal what the Egyptians achieved.

American tourists assemble at the Pyramids for the taking of the traditional photo.

An outsider might have difficulty distinguishing a Syrian from a Lebanese, or either of them from a Jordanian. But an Egyptian has certain well-defined characteristics. His Arabic is different, for one thing. His accent is distinctly Egyptian, and he uses words and phrases that are unassociated with other countries of the Middle East. Some of these terms date to the pharaohs; others have been derived from invading Europeans.

Egyptians are known to be a gentle and amiable people. Sharing, patience, and good humor are part of their character.

God has been worshipped in Egypt longer, perhaps, than in any other country of the world. Islam, the Muslim religion, is Egypt's official religion. Sadat's religion is an important part of his life and being, and he practices his faith devoutly. Five times a day he prostrates himself and worships God. (There is a dark callus at the center of Sadat's forehead, the result of bending his head to the ground in daily prayer.) Each time he prays, Sadat praises the Almighty and expresses his intention of being pleasing to God in word and deed.

"To me, God is everything that I cherish," Sadat has said. "We were taught that everything comes from God and God is everything."

Egyptian tradition from the time of the pharaohs has stressed loyalty to one leader. Anwar el-Sadat plays the role of leader to the hilt. His daily routine keeps him apart from mere bureaucrats and petty annoyances. Sadat is a man concerned with the forces and events that make for historic change.

Through the years, Sadat managed to stay in power by walking a political tightrope. He never permitted any military leader to get too strong. He never allowed any government figure to emerge as a person of influence. When anybody else gained independent popularity, he was removed from his job and usually made an "adviser to the president."

Although Sadat can be outgoing and very genial in public, those who know him best say that he is a quiet and introverted person. He has few friends. His closest is millionaire contractor Osman Ahmed Osman. One of Osman's sons is married to a daughter of Sadat's. But even Osman finds Sadat to be sometimes silent and withdrawn. He once said that he can be alone with Sadat for as long as two hours without speaking a single word.

Sadat keeps his important decisions secret. His ministers and even his wife often learn what he is planning from the daily newspapers. When he does arrive at a decision, he sticks to it no matter what. He is said to have a will of iron.

Seldom does anyone know what Sadat is thinking, not even his own family. "I go it alone," is the way he has expressed it. He says that the years he spent in prison, during the time the British controlled Egypt, turned him into a meditative man.

Sadat's wife, Jihan, spent the first twenty-five years of

President and Mrs. Sadat and their family.

their marriage devoting most of her time to the home and family. The Sadats have three married daughters—Lobna, Noha, and Jihan—and a son, Gamal, the youngest child. He is a graduate of the University of Cairo, a chemical engineer.

In 1974 Mrs. Sadat enrolled at Cairo University and earned a master's degree in Islamic literature. She later taught courses in that subject at the University two days a week. She also wrote and published poetry. In recent years she has become active in advancing women's causes in Egypt.

The favorite of Sadat's several presidential homes, called the Barrages, is on the eastern bank of the Nile in Cairo. Egyptian summers are torrid and temperatures in Cairo often spurt to above 100° F. (43° C.). The Sadats live in Alexandria in the summer, benefiting from the cooling winds that gust off the Mediterranean Sea. Winters are mild, with temperatures averaging between 55° and 70° F. (13° and 21° C.). During this time of the year, the Sadats live in Upper Egypt at Aswan.

The Nile at Cairo.

Sadat's daily routine provides ample time for meditation. He awakens every morning between eight and nine. He has a clock radio that he always sets himself, falling asleep and waking up to an all-music station in Cairo. On the table beside the radio he keeps a loaded pistol.

Sadat watches his diet carefully. His breakfast is usually a spoonful of honey. Sometimes he may also have papaya.

His health is another of his concerns. Because he believes he catches cold easily, he forbids air conditioning wherever he stays. The perspiration that results embarrasses him. An aid is always close by to hand him a fresh, white, folded handkerchief to wipe his brow.

Sadat is an elegant dresser, favoring British-style suits. He is rarely seen without a pipe.

Perhaps because he has had two mild heart attacks, Sadat does not work too hard. From about eleven he endures two hours of interviews and meetings.

Lunch is usually a bowl of soup. Throughout the day he drinks a variety of beverages—fruit juice, mint tea,

Alexandria beaches lure Egyptians during hot summer months.

and a European cola. As a Muslim, he never drinks liquor.

After lunch Sadat dons blue-and-white sneakers and takes a 2 $^1/_2$-mile walk. He has a rubdown from a masseur who is also one of his bodyguards. Next he takes a short nap.

Late in the afternoon Sadat may read official documents. He prefers, however, to have reports read to him.

Sadat's light supper usually consists of a dish of boiled food, such as pasta or rice. In the evening he and his family often watch a movie in their private screening room. Sadat himself prefers American Westerns.

Mrs. Sadat handles most family matters. "My father has enough problems," says Noha. "We wouldn't bore him with our own."

Besides Arabic, Sadat is fluent in English and German. He is an avid reader whose wide-ranging taste includes classical Islamic literature, the novels of Lloyd Douglas and Zane Grey, and the works of Arnold Toynbee and Harold Laski.

Sadat also writes. His two most noted books are *Revolt on the Nile*, published in 1957, and *In Search of Identity*, his autobiography, published in 1977. All proceeds from the autobiography go toward the educational and cultural development of the village of Mit Abul-Kum, where he was raised. He has said he would like to return to the village one day, to write and "lead my own life."

CHAPTER 2

THE ARAB REPUBLIC OF EGYPT (TO use its official name) is the most populous country in the Arab world and the second most populous (after Nigeria) on the continent of Africa. Egypt is also a big country geographically. Its borders enclose 386,972 square miles, an area about the size of Texas and New Mexico combined.

An infrared satellite photo of Egypt, which perceives the differences between desert land and land that can be farmed, tells another story. Viewed from space, the land that man can live on in Egypt is only 13,800 square miles in size, or an area less than half the size of the state of Maine.

The arable land of Egypt is shaped like a long-stemmed poppy. A thin strip of green land, from two to ten miles wide—the flower's stem—follows the Nile River north from the Sudan border. Between Cairo and the Mediterranean Sea—the flower's blossom—is the Nile Delta.

Ninety percent of the Egyptian people live in that area. Almost all of the rest of Egypt is brutal desert. Some twenty-five hundred years ago the Greek historian Herodotus described Egypt as "the gift of the river." That description fits as well today as it did then.

Egypt is a poor country with many problems. A high rate of population growth is one. The number of Egyptians has more than doubled in the past twenty years, from about twenty million in 1950 to well over forty million today. The population continues to increase at the rate of about one million every nine months.

(U.S. DEPARTMENT OF STATE)

The enormous increase in rural population has triggered a vast migration to the cities and towns. Cairo, a city of two million in 1950, has a population of more than eight million today. A thousand more people settle in the capital every day. Alexandria, the great port city on the Mediterranean, has grown at a similar rate, as have other cities.

"A municipal disaster" is how one recent visitor described the city of Cairo. Its slums are perhaps the worst in the world. People live on rooftops and in graveyards. Vast numbers of peasants spend their lives in one room, sleeping on the floor, taking their water from a public faucet, and using the street as a toilet. Many people go through their entire lives without once taking a bath.

Cairo's traffic jams are of monumental proportions. The streams of automobiles must contend with old and narrow streets and multitudes of carts drawn by horses or donkeys. A prospective passenger can wait hours for a bus. Most are so crowded the passengers must ride on the roofs. Bus doors never close. Other routine services— such as telephone, electric power, and garbage disposal— are all run down.

Rural life is vastly different. The poor peasants who work the land are called *fellahin*. Most live in crowded,

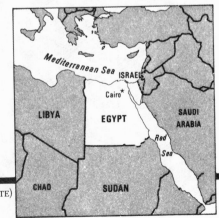

(U.S. DEPARTMENT OF STATE)

unsanitary villages. Houses are made of sun-dried brick with straw roofs. They have from one to three rooms.

Land is divided into small plots that are seldom larger than five acres in size and are rented from landlords. Each day is filled with constant toil. Precious water is raised from the Nile in the same way it has been for centuries. A cow or blindfolded water buffalo provides the power for a crude water wheel. There are some tractors, but not many. It is not economical to buy a tractor for only a few acres.

Cotton, beans, corn, onions, and potatoes are the principal crops. But the farmer has to use a portion of his land to raise alfalfa to feed his water buffalo. Egypt has to import about one-third of its wheat from the United States.

Goats and sheep are raised for meat and milk, and chickens for eggs and meat. Islam forbids its adherents to eat pork; thus, only non-Muslim farmers raise hogs. Cattle and water buffaloes provide some milk, but their chief use is as work animals.

During the early years of marriage, most *fellahin* men and their families live in their father's house. The women

Cairo, with the Al Azhar Mosque in the foreground.

(EGYPTIAN GOVERNMENT TOURIST OFFICE)

take care of the children, cook the family's meals, carry water, make butter and cheese, and raise chickens. The ordinary meals consist of *foul*, or beans. *Moulekieh*, a soup made from greens that grow amid the cotton plants, is a dish prepared for special days.

The childhood of the Egyptian *fellahin* was Anwar el-Sadat's childhood. He was born on December 25, 1918, in Mit Abul-Kum, a small village in the Nile Delta about sixty miles from Cairo. He was one of thirteen children. Anwar's father so much admired Kemal Atatürk, the co-founder of modern Turkey, that he named his sons after Turkish officers. Anwar's mother, from the Sudan, could neither read nor write.

When Anwar was still very young, his father, a military hospital clerk, was sent to the Sudan. With his father away, Anwar's grandmother became the head of the family. Although his grandmother was illiterate, she was one of the most respected members of the village. She could solve personal and family problems with her wisdom. She could cure the sick with herbal medicines based on ancient Arab recipes. When she passed through the

A view of the Nile at Aswan.

(EGYPTIAN GOVERNMENT TOURIST OFFICE)

streets of the village, with young Anwar trailing after her, barefooted, wearing his long white Arab dress over a calico shirt, men would rise as she approached and greet her warmly.

"How I loved that woman," Sadat has said of her.

Egypt was controlled by the British at this time. Although the British recognized Egypt as an independent state beginning in 1922 and Sultan Ahmed Fuad reigned as king, British troops remained in the country. There was constant strife between British soldiers and Egyptian

A country scene at Met Rahena, not fa from Cairo.

people. Young Anwar was well aware that his were troublesome times. At bedtime as he and his brothers lay stretched out on top of the family's huge mud-brick oven, along with their rabbits, their mother or grandmother would tell them stories of Egyptian patriots who had been imprisoned, beaten, or hanged by the British.

The tale that affected young Anwar the most told of Zahran, the hero of Denshway, a village only three miles away from Mit Abul-Kum. One day British soldiers were shooting pigeons in Denshway when a stray bullet set fire to a silo filled with wheat. When local farmers gathered to try to put out the blaze, a British soldier fired at them. The soldier ran away. The farmers ran after him. In the scuffle that followed, the soldier was killed.

The British wasted no time in seeking to avenge the soldier's death. Many villagers were arrested and promptly brought to trial. But even before the trials were completed and sentences handed down, the British started erecting platforms for hangings. A number of farmers were hanged. Other farmers were whipped.

Zahran was the hero of the tale. He was the first of the villagers to be hanged. The story told of Zahran's courage in battle, his pride, and how he walked with his head held high to the scaffold.

Young Anwar listened to the ballad night after night. His imagination played with the image. He often saw Zahran and lived his heroism. "I wished *I* was Zahran," Sadat has said.

Anwar was not so young that he did not realize that there was something wrong. How was it that the people of Denshway could be killed and beaten?

Anwar's grandfather could read and write, "a rare accomplishment," as Sadat himself has said. He wanted his son to be an educated man, and thus Sadat's father was sent to school. Since the British were occupying Egypt at the time, students were taught in English.

Anwar's father was the first of the villagers to complete grade school and receive a General Certificate of Primary Education. By so doing, he achieved high status in the village. Throughout his life, Mr. Sadat was known as "the *effendi*," a title of respect reserved for the well educated or members of the aristocracy. Anwar's grandmother was known as "the *effendi*'s mother."

Anwar's grandmother wanted him to receive an education as his father had. She enrolled young Anwar in a religious training school in the village, where he was taught to read and write. He also learned the Koran, memorizing it from front to back. The Koran is the sacred text of Islam, the foundation of Muslim religion, law, culture, and politics.

Anwar and the other students would sit on the classroom floor, each holding a notebook and writing with a reed pen, their only tools of learning. Anwar's long Arab dress had a big pocket. In the morning as he was leaving home for school, he would fill the pocket with bread crusts and pieces of dry cheese. He would munch on them during lessons or between classes.

Sheikh Abdul-Hamid was Anwar's teacher at the school. He helped to instill in Anwar a love of learning and the spirit of the Muslim faith.

When his Koranic schooling was completed, his grandmother enrolled Anwar in a Coptic school in Toukh, about a half a mile from the village where he lived. The Copts are descendants of the ancient Egyptians who were converted to Christianity in the A.D. 100s and 200s. Today slightly more than one million Egyptians still belong to the Coptic church. Sadat did not attend the Coptic school for a very long period. About all he remembers of the school is that he and his fellow students both loved and feared their teacher.

But school occupied only a part of young Anwar's time. At sunrise, before the broiling heat of the day, he and scores of boys and men would head out into the fields with their oxen, water buffaloes, and other beasts of burden. There were seeds to be sown, fields to be irrigated, and wheat, cotton, and dates to be harvested. Anwar would be assigned to take the cattle to drink from the canal. He would help in picking cotton or operate the ox-driven thrashing machine.

None of this was ever drudgery for young Anwar. Each family helped the others cultivate the land. In the winter the special canal that served Sadat's village was filled to overflowing, but only for about two weeks. During that period, all the land in the village had to be irrigated. The men of the village had to work quickly. They would toil on one person's land for an entire day, and the next day they would move on to another's.

The water was lifted from one level to another by means of the threads of an Archimedes' screw, or *tunbar*, which consisted of a spiral passage resting within an inclined tube. When the screw was turned, the water would be raised from the tube bottom to the top. The villagers used any *tunbar* that happened to be available. It didn't matter to whom it belonged. The main thing was to be sure that the entire village was irrigated by the end of the two-week period.

Such sharing affected almost every aspect of village life. Seldom did any one family have enough farm animals to plow and cultivate their fields. No matter. A buffalo would be borrowed. Or a plow. Or either would be cheerfully lent to a neighbor.

One day when Anwar was still attending the Coptic school, his father suddenly announced that the family was moving to Cairo. Thus the Sadats were made to endure the same anxieties that *fellahin* of the present day suffer when they exchange their placid village lives for the harshness of the city. Sadat himself did not take easily to his new life. In the village people depended on one another, indeed, belonged to one another. There was a spirit of mutual love. But in the city people were concerned with their wealth, power, and possessions.

Anwar's father chose a private school for him to attend. The family had barely enough money for food, and the fact that the school was not an expensive one was one of the chief reasons it was selected.

The new school was not far from Anwar's home, so he walked to it and back every day. In so doing, he passed Al-Qubbah, one of the royal palaces of King Fuad, the reigning monarch at the time. Sometimes Anwar and his friends would pluck a few apricots from the palace orchard. They would do so quickly and silently, their hearts pounding, for even to touch anything belonging to the king could spell death. Of course, Sadat did not know, nor did anyone else, that one day he would cross the threshold of the palace and sit on the very chair occupied by King Fuad and later by his successor, King Farouk.

When Anwar was twelve years old, he received his General Certificate of Primary Education, just as his father had. He and his brother Tal'at, the oldest of the Sadat boys, then went on to the Fuad I Secondary School.

By the standards of the Sadat family, it was a very expensive school to attend. Anwar's first tuition payment was £16 (about $38), a sum equal to his father's salary for an entire month. But Mr. Sadat gave his son the money. Anwar took it to school and made the payment.

Tal'at was given the same amount. But Tal'at took the money, ran away, spent it all, and then returned home to announce that he didn't care to continue his education.

Sadat has said that this incident might be taken as evidence of the workings of destiny. Sadat's father, because of his small income, would never have been able to keep both sons in school. And when the choice came as to which son could continue, Tal'at, because he was the eldest, would surely have been picked.

At secondary school Anwar was constantly reminded that he was a member of the Egyptian lower class. Some of his fellow students, the sons of government officials, came to school by car and dressed stylishly. At the school canteen they bought candies and chocolate. All Anwar could afford was a daily cup of milky tea.

Yet Anwar had no bitterness toward his wealthier classmates. He never wished to possess what they had. Instead he felt proud of the house and cattle the Sadats had owned and the fact that he belonged to the land.

Sadat had several heroes at this time, mostly individuals who were seeking to liberate their homelands. Mohandas K. (Mahatma) Gandhi was one. Several times the leader of the Indian National Congress, Gandhi was seeking to throw off the yoke of British rule and obtain independence for his country by means of nonviolent resistence. More than once he had been able to exact political concessions from the British by threatening "fasts unto death."

In 1932, when Sadat was fourteen, Gandhi passed through Egypt on his way to England. Articles about him and his struggle to oust the British from his country filled the Egyptian newspapers. Sadat fell in love with Gandhi and his image, and began to imitate him. He retreated to the roof of the Sadat home in Cairo. In imitation of Gandhi's practice of self-denial, Anwar refused all food and would not speak to anyone. Anwar's father finally persuaded him to give up the charade. It was winter and growing relatively cold. What benefit would it be to Egypt and to himself to get pneumonia, his father argued.

Kemal Atatürk, leader of the young Turk revolution in 1908, was another of Sadat's heroes. There was a picture of Atatürk in the Sadat home in Cairo, and Anwar's father described him as "a great man." Anwar's opinion of the Turkish leader was the same. Later, when Anwar studied the Turkish revolution and the role Atatürk played in it, he would be deeply influenced by H. C. Armstrong's book, *The Grey Wolf*, which delved deeply into the personality of the Turkish leader.

Mit Abul-Kum, the village where Sadat grew up, is changing. The primitive huts are being replaced by stone houses. The construction is being financed by royalties from Sadat's autobiography. He has erected a two-story villa at the spot where the Sadat family lived until he was six.

Sadat cherishes his peasant beginnings. The love of prayer, the willingness to endure hardship, a closeness to the earth, a native shrewdness—all of these facets of Sadat's character are rooted in Mit Abul-Kum. He returns there often to pray at the local mosque and mingle with the tradespeople.

Mit Abul-Kum gave Sadat his sense of being, of belonging. In his book he puts it this way: "...wherever I go, wherever I happen to be, I shall always know where I really am. I can never lose my way because I know I have living roots there, deep down in the soil of the village, in that land out of which I grew, like the trees and the plants."

His grandmother holds a special place in Sadat's memories of his early years. When I was preparing this book, I wrote to Sadat and asked him to cite the one person who most influenced his life. "...my grandmother, a simple countrywoman" was the person he cited.

In his letter to me, Sadat spoke of the enormous influence wrought by the legends and stories his grandmother narrated. The story of Zahran, Sadat said, became "deeply rooted in my heart."

While what was expressly stated in the legends was important, of even greater influence was what the legends implied. These stories of heroes and heroism, said Sadat, "turned out to be an embodiment of such virtues as honor, fidelity, and sacrifice." In the years to come, they would help to shape Sadat's thoughts and actions.

CHAPTER

3

IN 1936, WHEN HE WAS EIGHTEEN, Sadat received a General Certificate of Education, a document similar to a high school diploma. His hope was now to attend the Royal Military Academy. In order to be admitted to the military academy, however, one had to be sponsored by a person of influence and wealth, a *bey* or a *pasha*. But the Sadats knew no such person.

Then one day Anwar's father recalled that he had a friend, an officer with whom he served in the Sudan, who worked for Major General Ibrahim Khayri Pasha. Khayri, well known in Cairo social circles, was the chairman of the committee that examined military academy application forms. What could be better. A meeting was arranged.

It was an experience that would remain with Sadat throughout all of his life. He had never met a member of the ruling class before; and, of course, he had never been invited to such a person's home. Following instructions, Anwar and Mr. Sadat entered the home and waited in a hallway through which the *pasha* was to pass. After a few minutes, the *pasha* arrived. He looked at Sadat's father and said haughtily, "Oh, yes. You're the senior clerk of the Health Department, and that's your son who...I see ...all right, all right!" Then the *pasha* shot through a door, Mr. Sadat following.

Anwar felt a great loss of self-respect in being treated in such an offhand manner. It was a humiliation he did not forget. Indeed, some thirty years later, when Sadat was the speaker of the National Assembly, the same *pasha* came to see him concerning problems with property of his that was being taken by the government. Sadat reminded the *pasha* of their first meeting years before. "I owe you a lot," Sadat told him. "If it hadn't been for you, the revolution wouldn't have been possible."

At the Royal Military Academy, Sadat adopted Atatürk as his hero and became a student of the Turkish rebellion. He also studied Egyptian history, concentrating on the period that began with the British occupation of the country in 1882 and the tragic situation that followed.

Sadat fully realized that there were certain Egyptians who cooperated with the British and who even allowed themselves to be used by them. At Denshway, for example, when Zahran had been sentenced and tried, the judge, defense lawyers, and prosecuting attorneys—all had been Egyptians who were pro-British.

Sadat was married now. He had wed a girl from Mit Abul-Kum at a very young age. Early marriage was considered a necessity in the lives of Egyptian villagers in order for a young man to demonstrate his maturity. "Inevitable" is the word Sadat has used to describe the marriage.

Three children were born to the Sadats. The marriage was later dissolved. When Sadat became Egypt's president, the family would never be spoken of.

Sadat was impatient for the day when he would graduate from the military academy and begin to realize his dream. That day came in February, 1938.

Stationed at Manqabad, a small town in Upper Egypt, Sadat began to formulate plans to destroy the British and deliver Egypt from their rule. His room became the scene of nightly sessions in which he sought to stir up interest in his mission among his fellow officers. This group became the nucleus of the Free Officers' Association that was to seize power fourteen years later.

In the meantime, war clouds were gathering. Germany attacked Poland in September, 1939; and Britain and France, who had guaranteed Polish independence, declared war on Germany. Sadat saw the war as an opportunity of weakening the British position in Egypt.

After Italy entered the war on Germany's side, the British assigned the Egyptian army the task of helping defend the western desert aginst German and Italian forces advancing from Libya. Sadat saw a great paradox in this. To him, the enemy was Great Britain, not Germany. The Axis forces had not declared war on Egypt. Sadat's point of view was shared by many millions of Egyptians.

With each passing day the general feeling against the British mounted. In the summer of 1942, the armies of Field Marshal Erwin Rommel, commander of the German forces in North Africa, reached El Alamein, only sixty-five miles from Alexandria. Egyptians demonstrated in the streets of Cairo, chanting such slogans as "Advance, Rommel."

Sadat had no doubt that Rommel's armies would soon be at the gates of Alexandria. Once Alexandria had fallen, Cairo would be next. He called a meeting of his friends in the Free Officers' organization. They agreed that one of their group should be sent to Rommel informing him of their organization and that they, like Rommel himself, were fighting against the British. They were prepared to recruit an army to fight on Rommel's side. In addition they would provide Rommel with photographs and information concerning British installations in Egypt. In return, Sadat and his fellow officers wanted Rommel to promise that Egypt would be granted its independence once the war had ended and would not fall under German domination.

Unfortunately for Sadat's cause, the plane carrying the messenger, being a British aircraft, was shot down by the Germans. The offer never reached Rommel.

In the months that followed, Sadat made other efforts to try to collaborate with the Germans. He attempted to deliver a disgraced Egyptian general into German hands so he could advise the Germans as to how they could defeat the British. On his first try, the car Sadat and his cohorts were using broke down. When they made a second attempt, their airplane crashed on takeoff.

Sadat then began working with two German spies in Cairo who, unfortunately, were more interested in having fun than in spying. One of their escapades led to their arrest. One of the spies confessed, implicating Sadat.

In the middle of the night, British troops and King Farouk's political police went crashing into Sadat's house, hurtling the family out of its beds, breaking furniture and crockery, tearing the place to pieces. They were looking for Anwar. They found him and arrested him.

In October, 1942, following a court martial, Sadat was dismissed from the military service and imprisoned. As he was brought to his prison cell for the first time, Sadat conjured up an image of Zahran. He saw Zahran advancing toward death, unafraid, his head held high, happy at what he had done. While Sadat was not to be hanged, merely stripped of his rank and imprisoned, he felt he had achieved what Zahran had achieved—the joy of acknowledging a vast inner strength.

At one of the early meetings of the Free Officers', Sadat had met a burly, broad-shouldered young officer named Gamal Abdel Nasser. The son of a postal clerk, it would be Nasser who, as the president of Egypt, would overturn the monarchy and oversee the departure of the British. In 1939, when they first met, Sadat found Nasser a serious-minded and standoffish young man. Sadat was unsuccessful in his attempts to strike up a friendship with Nasser. Their relationship was one of mutual respect. When Sadat was sent to prison in 1942, it was Nasser who took over the leadership of the Free Officers' Association.

Sadat faced prison without fear or apprehension. But he was filled with anxiety about what might happen to his wife and children. Then he learned his fellow conspirators were going to pay his family the sum of $200 a month. He described this as balm to his soul.

Sadat remained in prison for two years. His cell was provided with a bed, blankets, a chair, and a small table. He was permitted to smoke, although a guard had to light his cigarettes since neither matches nor lighters were permitted in the cells. He was supplied with newspapers and books. He was given two recess periods a day in which he was allowed to walk within the prison walls for fifteen minutes. He prayed frequently.

Meanwhile, the tide of the war was beginning to change. Field Marshal "Monty" Montgomery had assumed command of the British forces and had cut Rommel's supply lines. In November, 1942, Montgomery launched a successful counterattack at El Alamein.

At about the same time, Sadat was transferred to another detention center, this one in Upper Egypt. He remained there for about a year, or until 1943. During that period, he taught himself German. He did it by reading a German novel, being helped by a fellow prisoner who could speak both German and Arabic. The first few times he tried the book, Sadat could read only four or five lines a day. He advanced to half a page and then a whole page in a day. After several months, he could read an entire chapter in a day. By the end of his prison stay, Sadat could speak and read German as well as a Berliner.

Many years later, as president of Egypt, Sadat visited Austria and made a speech in German. Secretary of State Henry Kissinger, who was originally from southern Germany, complimented Sadat on his German, saying that Sadat's northern accent was much closer to accepted German than his own.

Toward the end of 1943, Sadat, along with several other prisoners, was transferred to the Zaytun Detention Center near Cairo. While it was now easier for his family to visit him, he found life boring there. He and five other prisoners escaped. They were recaptured but escaped again.

For a year Sadat lived as a fugitive. He grew a beard and adopted the name of Hadji Muhammad. He worked at loading and unloading trucks. He later had a job hauling stone rubble from ships anchored in the Nile to a construction site. He worked from dawn to dusk. He went anywhere in Egypt he could find work.

On May 7, 1945, Germany surrendered, ending World War II in Europe and lifting the rule of martial law that had governed Egypt. Now Sadat was a free man. By September of that year, he was beginning to lead a normal life.

For Sadat "normal" meant resuming his terrorist activities, for he still burned with the desire to liberate his country from British rule. Sadat went to Nasser and demanded that the Free Officers' Association adopt terrorism as a political weapon. One of Sadat's proposals was to blow up the British embassy and everybody in it, including the ambassador. Nasser refused to take part in such a scheme.

Sadat then plotted the assassination of several political figures who were known for their pro-British views. He and his colleagues picked Egyptian Premier Mustafa Nahas Pasha as their first target. In the attempt on Nahas's life, a grenade hurled beneath Nahas's car was late in exploding. The premier escaped without injury.

The following year, 1946, Sadat and his followers plotted to assassinate Amin Osman Pasha, the Egyptian finance minister. An avid supporter of the British, Osman was fond of saying that the bond between Egypt and Britain was "as unbreakable as a Catholic marriage."

January 6, 1946, was the date on which the plot was to be carried out. Osman had just returned to Egypt from a trip to England and was scheduled to visit the headquarters of the Revival League, a political party he had formed. One of Sadat's conspirators, Hussein Tewfik, waited for Osman at the entrance to the headquarters building. As Osman approached, Tewfik called out,

"Pasha! Pasha!" When Osman turned, Tewfik fired, killing him.

Sadat felt that the assassination of Osman was a major accomplishment. Here was clear proof that the British were incapable of protecting those who supported them.

An Egyptian air force officer had seen the assassination; and his description of the killer led the police to Tewfik's home, and they arrested him. Within forty-eight hours after his arrest, Tewfik was trapped into making a full confession.

Shortly after, Sadat was arrested and jailed. When he would not confess his role in the assassination, he was thrust into a hellhole, Cell 54, of Cairo's Central Prison. Water oozed from the walls day and night. Armies of bugs were everywhere. There was no bed, only a fiber mat on an asphalt floor. Aside from the mat, the room was bare. Sadat was permitted little contact with the outside world, no newspapers, no radio.

One fifteen-minute walk was permitted each day when the prisoners were allowed to talk to one another. Their conversation dealt mostly with the unhumane conditions of the prison, particularly the filthy toilets. Sadat lived under such conditions for more than a year as he awaited trial.

The experience might have pushed a lesser man to the brink of insanity. But Sadat used the time for examining his mental and emotional states. He came to have a clear understanding of himself and what motivated him.

Later, when prison conditions improved and Sadat was permitted newspapers, magazines, and books, he began to read greedily, systematically educating himself.

He read more in English than in Arabic, and learned to speak the language. He also learned to read French.

Whenever he saw anything in print that appealed to him, he copied it into a notebook. He called it the Prison Notebook. He filled it with quotations from authors, Eastern and Western alike. Sadat still has the notebook.

The reading that he did helped him to broaden his mind and enrich his emotions. It helped him to know himself better. All in all, Sadat's prison experience brought him great peace of mind. The last eight months he spent in Cell 54 have been described by Sadat as among the happiest in his life.

CHAPTER

4

WHILE SADAT WAS PATIENTLY coping with the horrors of Cell 54, the attention of the world was being focused on the Middle East, specifically on a small, newly created nation on the eastern shore of the Mediterranean Sea. It had come into existence in 1948. Its name, of course, was Israel.

Israel made up most of the region once called Palestine. Both Judaism and Christianity originated in Palestine, and it was the locale of many events in the Bible. Muslims also considered Palestine to be a sacred place.

The territory that made up Palestine had been disputed for many thousands of years. In very early times, around 3000 B.C., that area of the world was known as the Land of Canaan. Semitic people called Hebrews left Mesopotamia (now part of Iraq) about 1900 B.C. and settled there. The Hebrews practiced a religion that centered around the belief in one God.

For some two hundred years, the Hebrews fought various other peoples of Canaan and neighboring lands. Eventually the Hebrews, who were organized by tribes, united under one king, Saul. David, Saul's successor, established Israel's capital in Jerusalem. His son, Solomon, succeeded David as king. He built in Jerusalem the first temple for the worship of God.

In 63 B.C. the Romans invaded Palestine and conquered it. The Romans were harsh rulers, and they were in constant conflict with the Jews.

During the time of Roman rule, Christ Jesus was born in Bethlehem. He began teaching a new religion and philosophy of life. In time, Christianity would spread throughout most of the world.

The constant strife between the Romans and the Jews led to an unsuccessful series of Jewish revolts. The Romans drove the Jews out of Jerusalem and named the area Palestine. For five hundred years, Palestine remained under Roman rule and later was part of the Byzantine Empire that followed it.

During the A.D. 600s, the Arabs surged across the Arabian desert and conquered Palestine. They were eager to spread the religion of Islam to every part of the world. The Muslim creed is simple: "There is no God but *the* God; Muhammad is His Messenger." The name of God in Arabic is *Allah*.

Muslims believe that God revealed His existence and voiced His message through a number of different men through the ages. These include Noah, Abraham, Joseph, Moses, Jesus, and Muhammad. Muhammad is the last messenger whom God sent. His message is set down in their holy book, the Koran.

Many Palestinians accepted Islam. But other countries, such as Egypt and Iraq, became more noted as centers of Muslim civilization.

The Arabs dominated Palestine for four hundred years. It was next conquered by the Seljuk people of Turkey. Within thirty years the Turks lost most of Palestine to the Christian Crusaders from Europe, who wanted to free the Holy Land from the Muslims. The Crusaders, in turn, were driven out by the Mamelukes, the military class that ruled Egypt at the time. In 1517 Palestine was conquered by the Ottoman Turks, and the country thus became a part of the Ottoman Empire.

Palestine became a terribly battered land, its cities crumbling, its farm lands neglected. The population was largely Arab, although there were small communities of Christians and Jews.

In the late 1800s European Jews, in order to live and die in the Holy Land, began to settle in Jerusalem and in other parts of Palestine. As oppression of the Jews worsened, the number immigrating to Palestine increased. This was the start of the Zionist pioneering movement that was to lead to the creation of the state of Israel. At the turn of the century, there were about a half-million people living in Palestine. Most were Arab peasants. About twenty-five thousand were Jews.

Palestine was a battlefield again in World War I, with the British fighting the Turks and driving them out of the country. Some of the Palestinian Jews fought on the side of the British.

In 1917 Britain issued the Balfour Declaration, which favored the creation of a Jewish homeland in Palestine. The League of Nations, like the United Nations of today, an international organization meant to promote world peace, later approved the Balfour Declaration.

Palestine's status as a nation began to change after World War I. Certain territories were taken from the defeated nations—Germany and Turkey—and placed under the administration of one or more of the victorious nations. This system of mandated territories, as it was called, was supervised by the League of Nations.

The British and French were given mandates to administer Arab lands that had been ruled by Turkey. Palestine, including the land that is now Jordan, was one of the Arab territories mandated to Britain.

During the 1920s and 1930s, many thousands of Jews settled in Palestine from different countries of the world. The Arabs in Palestine were angered by this immigration. They believed that Palestine was *their* homeland, and they wanted it to become an independent Arab state.

The resentment of the Arabs led to violence, rioting, and guerrilla fighting against the Jews. Meanwhile, World War II was approaching. As the Nazi terror swept Germany, huge numbers of German Jews fled their homeland and took refuge in Palestine.

The British, powerless to stop the clashes between the Arabs and Jews, gave in to Arab demands in 1939 and took measures to stop the Jewish immigration to Palestine. The Jews bitterly opposed the British decision.

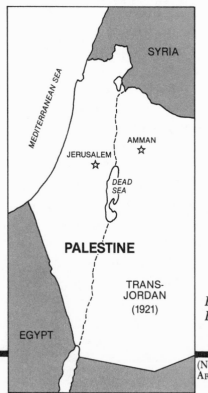

Palestine following British Mandate in 1920.

Many Jewish immigrants were brought to Palestine illegally. By now the Arabs and Jews were not only fighting one another, but they were fighting the British for control of Palestine.

In 1947 the British government, unable to find a solution to the problem, asked the United Nations to step in. That year the United Nations proposed the following:

• The country of Palestine would cease to exist. The territory within the borders of what was once Palestine would be divided into two states, one Arab state, the other Jewish. The Arab state, made up mostly of land on the West Bank of the River Jordan, became part of what was then known as Transjordan, now Jordan. The Jewish state became Israel.

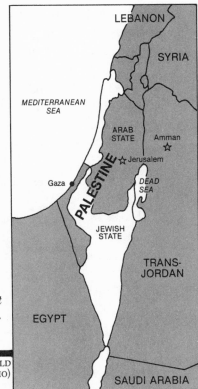

UN Partition Plan set these borders for Palestine.

(Neil Katine, Herb Field Art Studio)

•A small, rectangular piece of land on the Mediterranean Sea at the northeastern corner of Egypt, called the Gaza Strip, was taken by Egypt.

•The city of Jerusalem was to be internationalized, meaning that people of every nation were to be given access to the holy places.

The partition pleased the Jewish population of Palestine. But the Arabs, who made up the majority of the people affected, rejected it. They argued that the United Nations had no right to divide their land.

War seemed inevitable. Fear of the outbreak of hostilities led more than three hundred thousand Arabs to flee Palestine in the weeks before the United Nations plan was to go into effect. These refugees, at first no more than a hapless band of exiles, were to form the basis of a community that, in time, would number approximately four million displaced Arabs. They continued through the years to claim the land of Israel and the territory that included the West Bank of the River Jordan and the Gaza Strip as their birthright. As the years passed, their sense of injustice fired their anger. By the 1980s their plight would be known as the "Palestinian problem."

On May 14, 1948, British control of Palestine officially ended; and the state of Israel came into existence. The next day Israel was attacked by five Arab nations—Egypt, Iraq, Lebanon, Syria, and Transjordan. With the outbreak of war, another three hundred fifty thousand Palestinian Arabs took flight, abandoning their homes, farms, and shops.

The bulk of the Arab forces were drawn from the Egyptian army and the Arab Legion of Transjordan.

Egypt's military leaders had opposed the war. There was nothing to be gained and much to be lost.

Major-General Muhammad Naguib fought valiantly. But the war was a disaster for the Arab League and Egypt. Although their forces were far superior in number to the Israelis, they were soundly defeated by them.

From Cell 54, Sadat watched the Israeli air raids on Cairo. To his horror, the bombings occurred during the month of Ramadan, the holiest time of the year in the Muslim calendar. "God knows how I suffered at the time," he says in his book.

An armistice was signed on February 24, 1949, and the state of Israel became established. As a result of the war, Israel now controlled about one-half of the land that the United Nations had designated for the new Arab state, plus the western half of Jerusalem, which the United Nations had planned to put under international control. Jordan controlled the eastern half of the city.

There was great turmoil in Egypt as a result of the war. The people had been led to expect a quick and decisive victory. When it became known that the Egyptian forces were poorly equipped and poorly led, and thus outmatched by the smaller Israeli army, the peoples' hatred for the government and for the king deepened. There were demonstrations in the streets and one political upheaval after another.

It was during this period that Sadat won his release from prison. Late in 1948, he was finally tried for the role he was said to have played in the assassination of Amin Osman. The judge declared him not guilty, and he was set free.

He spent almost a month in solitude, recovering from his grim prison experience. Then a magazine began publishing a diary that he had kept while in prison, and Sadat went to work for the magazine as an editor. He quit that job to become business partners with a friend, an importer named Hassan Izzat.

One day on a visit to Izzat's home in Suez, Sadat met Izzat's wife. Her cousin Jihan Raouf happened to be visiting her.

Sadat was immediately attracted to the beautiful Jihan. The next day they went to the beach together. Jihan was a schoolgirl, the fifteen-year-old daughter of an Egyptian doctor who worked for the government and an English woman named Gladys, a former schoolteacher. Although she was a Muslim, Jihan had not been raised in the Muslim tradition of being submissive and helpless. From the time she was four until she was twelve, she attended a Christian missionary girls' school and, after that, a high school in Cairo.

At the time Sadat was penniless, once-married, and had just been released from thirty-one months in prison. He was from a peasant family. He was twice Jihan's age. And there was Sadat's skin color. Jihan once disclosed that her mother opposed the match because of Sadat's dark skin.

Despite their differences, they fell in love. Jihan has admitted she was attracted as much by Sadat's politics as by the man himself. Sadat proposed on September 29, 1948. Jihan's father accepted for her. They were married on May 29, 1949.

In the years that followed, Mrs. Sadat was to become one of her husband's closest advisers, concentrating her activities on the problems of the sick, the poor, and the disinherited. During the 1970s, she would embrace the cause of women's liberation and be described as one of Egypt's leading feminists.

Yet she readily admits that her husband is the head of the family. "If we give this pleasure to our husband," she once told *The New York Times*, "what do we lose?"

Early in 1950, Sadat's military commission was restored. Gamal Abdel Nasser was one of the first to call and congratulate him. Nasser was now president of the

Anwar and Jihan Sadat were married in 1949.

executive committee of the Free Officers', the organization within the army that was plotting to gain Egyptian independence. It was Nasser who held in his hands all of the threads to the plot.

Nasser told Sadat that the Free Officers' Association had grown significantly in size and influence. As if to demonstrate that influence, Nasser instructed Sadat to apply for a promotion from his rank of captain to that of lieutenant-colonel. Sadat did, and the promotion followed almost immediately.

Sadat's army superiors ordered him to act as a spy, reporting on the activities of suspected revolutionaries in the army, that is, to report on Nasser and his followers. Sadat could hardly believe his good fortune. He imme-

Sadat following his promotion to Lieutenant Colonel in 1952.

diately became a double agent, telling everything he knew, not to his army superiors, of course, but to Nasser and the Free Officers'.

Meanwhile tension was building. In a dispute over the control of the Suez Canal in Ismailia in January, 1952, fighting broke out involving fifteen hundred British troops and Egyptian auxiliary police. Forty-three Egyptians were killed.

The next day, January 26, 1952, savage riots erupted in Cairo against all foreigners. Much of central Cairo was set on fire, and many British-owned buildings were destroyed. Damage ran into the tens of millions of dollars. Weeks of unrest and instability followed.

Nasser had the Free Officers' poised to seize control of the government in November, 1952. But in mid-July of that year he learned the king was planning a countermove. They could wait no longer, Nasser realized. They would have to strike immediately.

At the time the final plans for the revolution were being drawn, Sadat was on military duty in Rafah, a town in the Gaza area. On July 21, 1952, Nasser summoned Sadat to Cairo, telling him the revolution was imminent. The next day, when Sadat arrived at the Cairo railroad station, no one was there to meet him. Thinking he had arrived ahead of schedule, Sadat went to his home.

His wife was surprised to see him. She asked him why he was in Cairo. It was a vacation, Sadat replied. That evening he took his wife to the movies. While Sadat was seated in a darkened theater, Nasser was seizing the reins of power.

When Sadat and his wife returned home, there were messages from Nasser. "Our project is tonight," one said.

Sadat said nothing to his wife but immediately donned his uniform, strapped a pistol to his belt, and left.

At the Army Command Headquarters, Sadat found Nasser. He told Sadat to telephone various unit commanders of the Free Officers' Association to determine whether everything was going according to plan. It was. The take-over was quick and bloodless.

Early on the morning of July 23, Nasser assigned Sadat to announce the birth of the revolution. It was thus Sadat who told the world from Broadcasting House in Cairo that the Free Officers had seized control of the government and were demanding the resignation of King Farouk. Immediately the streets of Cairo began to fill with joyous people. The king left Egypt three days later.

Egypt's first president was Major-General Muhammad Naguib, a popular figure; but it was generally recognized that the real power in the country rested with Gamal Abdel Nasser. Two years later Nasser became Egypt's ruler in name as well as in fact, replacing Naguib.

Nasser cracked down on the old society. Many army officers were dismissed, and former associates of the king were arrested. Nasser limited land ownership to 200 acres and ordered that larger plots be redistributed to the peasants. As for the British "occupation" of the country, that ended with the Anglo–Egyptian Agreement of 1954.

While Sadat had been named to the Revolutionary Command Council of the Free Officers' Association and served in a number of other posts, Nasser did not give him a leading role in the new government. Sadat became editor of *Al Gomhouriva*, the government newspaper, and frequently authored articles for it that were strongly anti-American. Secretary of State John Foster Dulles was one of his favorite targets.

Sadat became secretary general of the Islamic Congress, an organization that was intended to rally the world's four hundred million Muslims in support of Nasser. But the Congress never really accomplished very much. From 1954 to 1956, Sadat was minister of the state, and in 1957 he was appointed secretary general of the National Union.

As president, Nasser's most ambitious project was to build a High Dam on the Nile River at Aswan. Such a dam was considered essential to control the waters of the Nile so that the area open to cultivation could be increased. In addition, the dam would enable water to be released for agricultural purposes in periods of the year when the river was normally low.

At the beginning of 1956, it was agreed that the initial construction work on the dam would be financed by the World Bank, the United States, and Great Britain. But this was a period of the Cold War between the United States and the Soviet Union, a rivalry that was just short of armed conflict. Nasser and Egypt got caught in the middle of the Cold War.

After Nasser purchased arms from Czechoslovakia and then, in 1956, recognized Communist China, American legislators began to feel that Egypt was being drawn into the Communist orbit. As a result, the United States withdrew its offer to help build the Aswan Dam. John Foster Dulles, the United States Secretary of State, declared that the Egyptian economy was bankrupt, and the country could never be expected to make the billion-dollar construction project a success. The World Bank and Great Britain also withdrew their support.

Nasser was livid. He reacted by seizing the Suez Canal Company, which was owned jointly by the British and French. He then announced that all tolls collected from the use of the Canal would be used to finance the construction of the Aswan Dam.

Overnight Nasser thus became a hero in the eyes of the Egyptian people. Sadat has called the take-over of the Suez Canal the turning point in the history of the revolution. As he saw it, the Egyptian people could at last enjoy a moment of proud achievement after a century of humiliation and oppression at the hands of the British.

But Sadat also had misgivings about the decision. He felt it could lead to war.

Sadat's estimate of the situation was soon proven correct. Britain and France plotted to attack Egypt with the object of overturning Nasser's rule. They hoped this would lead to their regaining control of the Suez Canal.

In October, 1956, in a secret meeting near Paris, Britain and France agreed that Israel should initiate the attack. The Israelis needed little urging. Egypt had blocked Israeli ships from using the Suez Canal and had also taken steps to prevent them from entering the Gulf of Aqaba, an arm of the Red Sea leading to southern Israeli ports.

On October 29, 1956, Israel invaded the Gaza Strip and the wedge-shaped Sinai Peninsula, a huge—23,444-square-mile—expanse of barren desert between the Suez Canal and Egypt's border with Israel. The Israeli troops and armored units moved with power and precision, quickly capturing huge chunks of Egyptian territory.

The British and French joined in. Planes from Britain and France bombed Port Said at the Canal's northern end, and the city fell to paratroopers.

Several warnings from the United States and the Soviet Union brought a truce on the tenth day of the war. The United Nations then intervened, demanding that British, French, and Israeli troops leave Egypt. By December, 1956, the last British and French troops were out. Israeli forces withdrew by March, 1957. The United Nations sent a ten-nation, peace-keeping force to police the border between Egypt and Israel. A United Nations salvage team cleared the Canal. It was reopened in March, 1957, under Egyptian management.

All of the Arab nations rallied to Nasser's support, and his popularity soared. For someone who had lost a war, Nasser had come off surprisingly well. The next time he would not be so fortunate.

CHAPTER 5

NOT LONG AFTER THE FREE OFFI- cers' had taken over the government, Nasser, having assumed full control, asked the Revolutionary Command Council this question: "What sort of philosophy are we going to adopt— dictatorship or democracy?".

Sadat and all the other members of the Revolutionary Command Council voted for a dictatorship. Nasser was the only one to vote for a democracy.

There is* great irony in what actually happened. Decades later, when Sadat became president, he would turn out to be a democrat. Nasser, on the other hand, almost from the first moment he took office, was the consummate dictator.

No one seemed to mind, however. Nasser brought visions of prosperity to Egypt. And more than that, he beguiled the Arab world, offering hope that the glories of ancient times might be recaptured.

A long and radiant success for the Arabs began in the seventh century with the appearance of Muhammad and the religion of Islam. Under Muhammad's urging, the Arab people forged an empire greater in size than that of Alexander the Great or of any of the conquests of the Caesars. The Arab armies defeated the Byzantine and Persian armies, carrying Islam as far west as Spain and southern France and as far east as India and the Chinese border.

During this period of the Dark Ages, the Arabs were the custodians of world science and culture. But after Muhammad's ascension heavenward, competing spiritual leaders drained Arab power with their feuds. And when Portuguese explorers discovered new routes to the Orient around Africa, the importance of Arab ports diminished. By the sixteenth century, the Ottoman Empire dominated the Arabs. Later, European nations held sway in the Arab world.

Nasser's determination to rid the Arab world of foreign domination and weld the Arab nations into a powerful unit imparted to the people of Egypt and to much of the rest of the Arab world a sense of national price reminiscent of a time some four hundred years before.

In February, 1958, Egypt and Syria, at Nasser's urging, combined to form a new nation, the United Arab Republic. Nasser was elected its president. Later, Yemen,

An official portrait of Sadat from the early 1960s.

a small republic at the southwestern corner of the Arabian Peninsula, joined the union. Syria was never happy under Nasser's leadership, however, and withdrew from the United Arab Republic in 1961. Later that year Nasser dissolved Egypt's agreement with Yemen. Egypt, however, kept the United Arab Republic as its name until 1971.

Throughout his regime Nasser was wary about allowing anyone to acquire too much power. When a military officer or a cabinet minister sought to advance his cause too boldly, his career would suddenly be short-circuited.

But this never happened to Sadat. While he remained a loner, he was always wholly loyal to Nasser. He remained in the background, never disputing Nasser in public and rarely in private. So agreeable was Sadat that Nasser sometimes referred to him as "Colonel Yes-Yes."

Throughout this period Sadat relied on his remarkable patience. Occasionally he and Nasser would quarrel. Sometimes the quarrel would be the result of a difference of opinion. At other times the disagreement would be triggered by some member of Nasser's inner circle. It was known that Nasser liked to listen to gossip.

Whatever the argument, Sadat would not seek to win it. He would simply melt into the shadows for awhile. After several weeks, Nasser would call and ask how he had been and why he hadn't been in touch with him. Sadat would answer that he thought Nasser had been busy with affairs of state, and he didn't wish to impose on the leader's time. Thereupon the two men would meet and continue their relationship as if nothing had happened.

From time to time Sadat's old brashness and impulsiveness surfaced. As a member of the Egyptian delegation to the Asian–African Bandung Non-Alignment Conference in 1955, where nations whose sympathies were with neither the Soviets nor Americans came together as a third international force, Sadat's insolence was so unsettling to Muslim leaders that Nasser ordered him home. As speaker of the Egyptian National Assembly, Sadat went to Moscow in 1961 and engaged in a shouting match with Nikita Khrushchev, the Soviet premier at the time, when Khrushchev attacked Nasser for persecuting Egyptian Communists. Sadat was also guilty of playing the role of a warmonger, delivering speeches in which he baited the Israelis.

Sadat traveled widely during this period. He visited remote corners of Egypt, getting to know the people more deeply than ever. He traveled all over the Muslim world. He went to Yugoslavia and Mongolia. He visited the United States in 1966, an official guest of the American government. He met with President Lyndon Johnson. He toured Disneyland.

But mostly Sadat bided his time. He waited.

Sadat tours U.S. Capitol in 1966.

Nasser was never able to coax the Arab states into political accord. They were united on only one matter, their hatred of Israel.

These animosities lead to war again in 1967. In June of that year, Nasser took Syria's word that Israel was preparing an attack and ordered United Nations peace-keeping forces out of Egypt.

Egypt then began massing troops in the Sinai along the Israeli border. Syria and Jordan also built up their forces along their borders with Israel.

The breaking point was at hand. Israel had developed the port of Eilat on the Gulf of Aqaba, creating an alternate to the Suez route to Asia and East Africa. When Nas-

The Sadat family in New York in 1966.

(PRESS & INFORMATION BUREAU, EMBASSY OF THE ARAB REPUBLIC OF EGYPT)

ser closed the Gulf of Aqaba to Israeli shipping, war followed immediately.

On June 5, 1967, as the first shots were being fired, Egyptian Field Marshal Abdel Amer flew off on a tour of inspection of Egyptian units in the Sinai. Egyptian antiaircraft batteries and installations of surface-to-air missiles were ordered to withhold their fire while his plane was in the air.

It was during this period that the first wave of Israeli Mystere and Mirage supersonic fighters took off from secret bases, swept out over the Mediterranean, banked, and then came back again from the north to devastate sixteen Egyptian airfields and the aircraft sitting on them. By midmorning almost four hundred Egyptian aircraft had been put out of commission. Similar attacks were made on Syria and Jordan.

The outcome of the war was never in doubt after the first few hours. Brigadier General Mordecai Hod, commander of the Israeli air force, called it a victory beyond his wildest dreams.

Sadat entered Amer's office not long after the field marshal had returned from his inspection tour and was just beginning to learn the dimensions of the disaster that had befallen the Egyptians. "Good morning," said Sadat. Amer's eyes were glazed, and he didn't seem to hear. "Good morning," said Sadat again. After another minute, Amer returned the greeting. Others in the room then explained to Sadat that the Egyptian air force had been wiped out on the ground.

When Nasser arrived, Amer put the blame on the Americans, saying it was planes of the U. S. air force that were responsible. Nasser knew the accusation was non-sense.

With the Israelis in complete control in the air, it was an easy matter for their ground forces to overrun the Gaza Strip and the Sinai, sweeping all the way to the Suez Canal in a matter of days. Amer aided the cause of the Israelis by ordering an Egyptian withdrawal, an order Sadat branded as being, in effect, an order to commit suicide.

At first there were reports that Israeli troops had crossed the Canal to the west bank, but they proved untrue. There was really no need for them to make the crossing. They had done what they set out to do, and they had done it with terrible swiftness. The Egyptians had been defeated within a space of six days. The conflict has since become known as the Six-Day War.

Besides Egyptian land, Israeli forces seized all of Jordan's territory west of the River Jordan. The Israelis considered this land to be of critical importance because it penetrated to the very center of their country and included Jordan's half of the city of Jerusalem.

Syria lost the Golan Heights to the Israelis. Although rugged and barren, the Golan Heights were valuable as a strategic barrier between the two countries. Israel's size was now three times what it had been in 1948, the year of its founding.

As the biggest and supposedly most powerful of the Arab nations, the defeat was particularly humiliating to Egypt. Nasser's pride had been dealt a crippling blow. Only a few days before, the world had waited tensely and expectantly for what he had to say. Now he was a laughingstock.

Nasser's appearance changed drastically. His eyes turned dull. His smile no longer dazzled. His face and hands took on a sickly pallor. Death seemed to be stalking him.

A period of intense suffering followed for the Egyptians as they agonized over their defeat. Sadat described himself as being overwhelmed by the debacle. He shut himself off from the world for several weeks so he would not have to listen to the abuse and denunciations being heaped upon the Egyptian armed forces.

It was being said that the Egyptians were not fit for battle, that Egyptian soldiers should not even attempt to recover land that had been taken by the Israelis, that no effort should be made to restore the national honor.

Israel's expanded borders after 1967 War.

(NEIL KATINE, HERB FIELD ART STUDIO)

Sadat could not bring himself to accept those opinions. Such beliefs, he knew, could mean the eventual destruction of the Egyptian people. Their lot might come to be similar to that of the Indians of North America, he thought.

Sadat began a personal investigation to establish how the Egyptian foot soldier had handled himself during the fighting. An Egyptian brigade had launched a counterattack on June 7, the second day of the fighting. Sadat sought out and questioned members of the brigade. It didn't take him long to learn that the brigade's effectiveness had been destroyed by confusion among the commanding officers, not cowardice or the lack of fighting spirit on the part of the foot soldiers. Conflicting orders had been issued to the brigade. Indecision had been rampant. As a result, the brigade had been forced to cover many hundreds of miles of desert terrain, which put a severe strain on its tanks and other vehicles. Despite all this, the brigade had lost only about twenty tanks—one-fifth of its total number—and had still been able to shoot down seven enemy aircraft.

After his investigation Sadat came to the conclusion that the Egyptian soldier did not lack for training, weapons, or fighting ability. His findings confirmed what others were saying. The Egyptian soldier, often recruited from the peasant class, was obedient and hard fighting. He seldom was capable of taking action on his own, however, and could be confused by sophisticated weapons. But the Egyptian soldier would fight bravely when well led.

Leadership was the profound problem. For centuries Egypt had been dominated by foreign powers, and its army officers were rarely Egyptians. From 1882 to 1936, when the British were in control, the Egyptians were prevented from forming an effective army of their own. The officer corps that was permitted to exist was lesss than professional, being made up of pashas' sons, most of whom spent their time playing polo.

The situation had began to change in 1936 when, for the first time, the peasant and middle classes were admitted to the Royal Military Academy. These young men saw in military life an opportunity for good pay and a wide range of other benefits. Officers, for example, often held high government posts or were directors of private companies in addition to their responsibilities to the military.

Nasser was aware of this problem. He had ordered his officers to resign their commissions if they wished to remain in their civilian jobs. But by the time he had issued the order, it was too late. With money and privilege as their twin objectives, the Egyptian officer corps had grown fat.

Field Marshal Amer had been popular with the officers because he had pampered them. But in combat they often acted in a pitiable manner. There were many cases where, in battle, they had abandoned their troops and run.

As a result of the Six-Day War, the Egyptians lost much more than land. They lost their sense of honor; they lost their self-esteem. Their wretched showing would lead to years of public scorn and humiliation. Out of this would come self-contempt and, eventually, an even deeper hatred for Israel and a thirst for revenge.

CHAPTER

6

FROM THE TIME OF EGYPT'S STUN-
ning defeat in the Six-Day War in
1967, Nasser's health steadily de-
teriorated. He suffered from dia-
betes, a disease that impairs the
body's ability to use sugar. He fell
victim to another illness that
caused tortuous pain in his legs,
pain so bad that he would lock himself in his bedroom
and scream at the top of his lungs.

In September, 1969, Nasser suffered a heart attack. Although he recovered, doctors told him he needed complete rest. They told him that physical exercise or mental
stress could prove fatal. The problems of Egypt were Nasser's life. He could not be asked to slow the frantic pace of
his life any more than a fish could be asked to stop swimming.

But Nasser knew he was treading on dangerous
ground. One December day in 1969, not long before he
was to leave for a conference in Morocco, he announced
to Sadat that he was going to appoint him vice-president.
Nasser said he did not want to leave behind a vacuum.

Sadat's brow wrinkled. He replied that he didn't want
to be named vice-president. He pledged his continued
support and suggested the title "Presidential Adviser"
might be suitable.

"No!" said Nasser. "You will be sworn in tomorrow."

When Sadat arrived at Nasser's home the next day to
drive him to the airport, Nasser asked him to be sworn in.
Sadat agreed. When they arrived at the airport, Nasser
announced publicly that Sadat was now his vice-
president.

In the months that had followed the Six-Day War, Nasser ordered striking changes in the Egyptian army. He appointed General Muhammad Fawzi to replace Field Marshal Amer (who later committed suicide). He also began getting rid of officers who were incompetent, sometimes purging more than a hundred of them at a time.

Illiterate soldiers were discharged, their places taken by high school and even university graduates. Officers were required to make the army a career. Higher pay was offered to attract better officers. A much greater emphasis was placed on organization and discipline.

By 1970 the Egyptian army was of much higher quality. It then numbered about a quarter of a million men, of whom about ten thousand formed a tough commando force. These troops had begun making periodic raids across the Canal into the area occupied by Israeli forces and had engaged the Israelis in fierce combat on more than one occasion.

But Egypt's military situation was complicated by what was now an enormous Soviet presence, encouraged by Nasser. There were between twelve and fifteen thousand Russian "advisers" in Egypt, consisting of engineers, missile technicians, and pilots. They were assigned to every Egyptian military unit.

The Russians also were providing Egypt with weapons. The weapons, however, were always defensive in nature. Sadat has stated that the Soviets had no wish for Nasser to fight another war. It supplied Egypt with weapons more as a courtesy gesture than anything else, in recognition of the country's anti-American stand. The Soviet Union, said Sadat, never intended for the weapons to be used.

There were always serious problems in dealing with

the Russians, a condition that Sadat fully realized. For example, whenever an order for arms was placed, the Russians would never specify when delivery was to be made. They always fixed the time themselves.

Egyptian military leaders realized that air defense was their greatest weakness, a fact the Six-Day War had confirmed all too clearly. But Nasser's efforts to obtain sophisticated surface-to-air missiles from the Soviets were less than successful. A year went by. Then another. Still no missiles. In January, 1970, Israeli planes bombed a factory on the outskirts of Cairo, killing more than seventy workers. Nasser cried out again for the missiles he had been promised. Two months later they were finally delivered.

The Egyptians were also promised the advanced TU-16 Russian aircraft, which they never received. Egyptian inquiries about delivery dates were ignored.

More and more it became obvious to Sadat that Nasser had painted himself into a corner. He had broken relations with the United States and with many nations of western Europe in order to curry favor with the Soviet Union. Now that the Soviets were proving unreliable, Nasser had nowhere to turn.

In the summer of 1970 Nasser paid a long visit to Moscow, hoping to pressure the Russians into sending Egypt a new "deterrent" weapon. When Nasser arrived home, Sadat asked him whether he had been successful. Nasser, shaking his head from side to side, answered with two English words: "Hopeless case."

The treatment that Nasser received at the hands of the Soviets crushed him, Sadat believes. It caused a deterioration in his morale and, eventually, his health.

In September, 1970, Nasser called an Arab Summit Conference into session in Cairo. The kings or presidents of every Arab country attended.

Much bitterness was evident among the conference participants. General Muammar al-Qaddafi of Libya, and Yasir Arafat, the head of the Palestine Liberation Organization, were each guilty of emotional outbursts that caused tempers to flare.

All of this was a great burden on Nasser's nervous system. As the conference was drawing to a close, he was exhausted. Nevertheless, he went to the airport to extend a personal good-bye to each of the Arab leaders. The last to leave were King Faisal of Saudi Arabia and the amir of Kuwait. After Faisal's departure, Sadat noticed that Nasser's face was ashen and he walked shakily. He suggested that Nasser go home to rest and offered to see off the amir of Kuwait. But Nasser refused.

When the amir boarded his plane, Nasser could not move at all. He stood in front of the aircraft, sweating heavily, his face the color of chalk. A limousine was brought to where Nasser was standing. He was helped into the car and driven home.

Later that afternoon Sadat received a telephone call from Nasser's secretary asking him to come to Nasser's home right away. When he arrived, he was shown into Nasser's bedroom. What he saw made him gasp. The Egyptian leader was in bed surrounded by doctors, the bedcover over his face. The doctors told Sadat that Nasser had died of a heart attack about an hour before.

Sadat lifted the bedcover. Nasser looked as though he might only be asleep. "I put my cheek against his but did not feel the chill of death," Sadat says in his book. He turned to the doctors and said, "It's not true. What you're saying is wrong. It can't be right!"

The doctors assured Sadat that they had done all they could possibly do. Sadat burst into tears.

Nasser's death triggered a great outpouring of grief throughout the Arab world. In Beirut, Lebanon, tens of thousands of Arabs poured into the streets. They lit funeral bonfires, shot off rifles, and exploded dynamite charges. The frenzy lasted three days. Fourteen people died. In countless other towns and villages of the Middle East, mock funerals were held with weeping men carrying empty coffins, while huge throngs followed, wailing in their sorrow.

Cairo was shaken to its foundations. Peasants descended upon the city in great throngs during the days before the funeral, which was witnessed by more than five million people. They stood two hundred deep in some places. They hung from trees and lampposts. "Nasser is God's beloved," they chanted. "Nasser is not dead."

These striking photos of Sadat were taken not long before his selection as preside

A gun carriage pulled by six black horses carried Nasser's coffin. It was followed by a troop of cavalrymen. Six military bands played Chopin's *Funeral March*. Twenty-seven heads of state and twenty-two other foreign delegates assembled behind the gun carriage.

As the gun carriage began to move, the crowd surged forward to engulf the procession. Police had to beat back the mourners with whips and bamboo sticks. It took about an hour to move the first one hundred yards. Eventually the coffin had to be transferred to an armored car that nudged its way through the throng to the burial crypt.

Egypt's constitution allowed up to sixty days for the country to select a successor to President Nasser, but only nine days were needed. On the ninth day, 353 members of the Egyptian National Assembly formally elected Sadat as the new leader of the country. The following week, when the population voted in yes-or-no balloting,

...s ratified by a people's plebiscite in October 1970.   (UNITED PRESS INTERNATIONAL)

Sadat received a 90.4 percent "yes" vote from seven million Egyptians. Shortly after, he was sworn into office for a six-year term.

According to some sources, Sadat was elected to succeed Nasser because no one strongly liked or disliked him. He was regarded as something of a neutralist. He also agreed to share power substantially.

Sadat was anything but a popular figure at the time. An American newspaper correspondent in Cairo recalled attending the movies not long after Nasser's death. During the newsreel, when Nasser's image flashed on the screen, the audience cheered wildly. Sadat's appearance was greeted mostly by silence, but there were some catcalls and derisive whistles.

In some quarters it was worse. Sadat was something of a public joke. He was ridiculed for his peasant background and his brown skin. He was dismissed as a "caretaker," an individual who would soon be replaced by someone more powerful. The only picture ever to be seen in public buildings was Nasser's, the dead hero, a slash of black across one corner.

Sadat's stock was not much higher with leaders of the American government. At the time of Nasser's death, President Richard Nixon had sent Elliot Richardson to Egypt as a special envoy to express America's sympathies. When Richardson arrived back in Washington, he submitted a report saying that Sadat would not remain in power for more than eight weeks.

To a great extent, Sadat was president in name only. The *real* power in Egypt was in the hands of three other government officials who considered themselves Nasser's rightful heirs. They expected Sadat to do whatever they told him. These men were Sami Sharaf, the presidential affairs minister; Sharawi Gomah, interior minister; and Ali Sabri, who was in charge of Egypt's Russian-built air defense system.

During his years as Egypt's president, Nasser had not trusted anyone. He often played one government official against the other, keeping a careful record of the misdeeds of each. He used Sharaf as his chief spy. The man thrived by bugging his rivals' living quarters and betraying his friends.

Gomah was no better. He controlled the police and the government's investigative branch, its CIA. He was a specialist in snooping devices, which he purchased from all parts of the world. At the same time that Sadat was

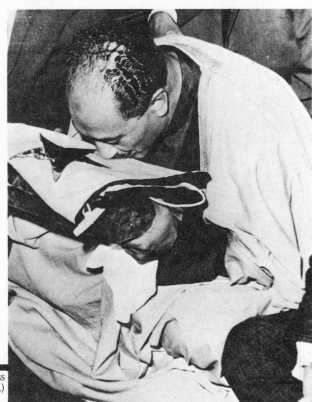

Sadat kisses an Egyptian flag during noon prayers at his home village in October 1970, not long after becoming president of Egypt.

taking over the reins of the government, Gomah was preparing for *his* own eventual inauguration.

Ali Sabri was Egypt's chief contact with the Soviet Union, a former prime minister and minister of presidential affairs. Although judged by many to be the most powerful man in Egypt, Sabri was anything but a popular figure and was distrusted by the military.

Sadat simply ignored his dangerous rivals at first. Instead, he began working diligently to change his image. He put an end to the seizure of public property, which had not been uncommon during the period of Nasser's rule; and many Egyptians were able to reclaim land that had been taken from them. The secret police were far less in evidence, and open criticism of the government was allowed again.

The people of Egypt came to like Sadat's style. He did not govern in a frenzy, as Nasser had. He was cool and confident. After becoming president, Sadat moved into a mansion in the Giza district of Cairo on the west bank of the Nile. He preferred spending as much time as possible with his wife, their three daughters and son, Gamal, as well as with their two collies, Lassie and Whip. In televised speeches to the nation, Sadat was friendly and informal, even chatty. One of them he dubbed a "heart-to-heart" talk.

Sadat also visited army installations and talked to the officers and listened to their complaints. Army officials pledged to support Sadat should there be a power struggle.

Sadat's stock soared with the Egyptian people. The jokes about him were forgotten. In June of his first year in office, King Faisal of Saudi Arabia paid a state visit to

Egypt. In Cairo thousands of people stood for hours in temperatures of over one hundred degrees, waiting to catch a glimpse of the two leaders. People in the street stopped to applaud Sadat's car, even when they weren't sure Sadat was in it.

Sadat began to feel confident that he had achieved widespread popularity among the Egyptian people. But these were tension-filled days for him and his family. Several members of the Egyptian National Assembly went to Mrs. Sadat and told her to warn her husband of a plot against him. When she told him, Sadat merely shrugged. Mrs. Sadat was infuriated by his calmness.

"Who is with you?" she asked him. "Not the Minister of Defense. Not the Minister of the Interior, and not the Minister of Information. Not one of them."

Don't worry," Sadat said, "God is with us."

Sadat had been planning a trip to Alexandria, but he learned that the plotters were planning to assassinate him on his way there. He cancelled the trip.

That night was one of great anxiety. Sadat always kept a pistol beside his bed. His wife asked him to lock the bedroom door. "That way," she said, "if they come, you will be ready with your pistol."

Mrs. Sadat spoke to their oldest daughter, Lobna, age seventeen, and suggested she sleep at a friend's house. Lobna refused. "If they blow up the house," she said, "do you think I would be happy living without my father and mother?" She took a book and went upstairs to bed.

Sadat's son, age fifteen at the time, got out a small-caliber hunting rifle he owned and insisted on being his father's bodyguard.

Army trucks arrived later that night bringing soldiers

to guard the Sadat home. The night passed without incident.

The next day Sadat moved decisively. He had all those he felt to be disloyal to him arrested and jailed, including Sharaf, Gomah, and Sabri, accusing them of corruption, embezzlement, and bribery. Most of the officials who were arrested were held in the basement of a government building, where they were made to sleep on blankets on the floor.

Other officials were demoted or forced to resign. More than three hundred individuals were affected. Sadat swept the government clean and appointed new officials.

Now that he was in command, both in name and fact, Sadat attempted to come to terms with problems that had been shunted aside during Nasser's regime. He had seen a report issued in the United States not long before Nasser's death. It said that with the increased consumption that would result from Egypt's mushrooming population, the country's economy would be reduced to zero by 1972.

Sadat realized that the report gave a true analysis of the situation. When he summoned Dr. Hassan Abbas Zaki, Minister of Finance and Economy, and asked for a rundown on the financial state of the nation, the finance minister told Sadat that the country was on the brink of disaster. The treasury was empty, the country almost bankrupt, said Saki.

The problem was so severe that the government might soon be unable to pay the salaries of civil employees and members of the armed forces. If that happened, Sadat asked himself, would Egypt collapse?

In the field of foreign policy, Sadat realized that his problems were almost as bad. Outside the Arab sphere,

Egypt had diplomatic relations with the Soviet Union—
and with no one else.

Sadat moved boldly in solving the "Russian problem."
Nikolai Podgorny, the president of the Soviet Union, and
a delegation of top Soviet officials visited Sadat not long
after he had taken full control. The Russians were upset.
When Sadat had cleaned house and ousted those who
were plotting against him, a number of government officials who were close friends with the Russians had been
arrested and imprisoned. A political cartoon showed Podgorny meeting Moscow's friends in Egypt—and they
were all dressed in prison uniforms.

Podgorny asked Sadat, as evidence of his good inten-
tions, to enter into a Treaty of Friendship and Cooperation with the Soviet Union. Under the treaty terms, the
Soviets agreed to supply Egypt with arms and munitions.
In return Egypt was to agree not to resume a shooting
war with Israel without Russia's approval.

During the meeting with Podgorny, Sadat declared he
was not happy with the way the Russians had been treat-
ing the Egyptians. He complained that the weapons the
Egyptians had been receiving were unacceptable in terms
of both quantity and quality. As a result, the Egyptian
military machine lagged far behind that of the Israelis.

Podgorny asked for four days, promising all the
weapons would be shipped in that time. That was in
May, 1971. Sadat waited through June, July, August,
and almost all of September. The weapons never arrived.
His letters to Moscow went unanswered.

That summer the Communists moved to take over the
government of the Sudan, Egypt's neighbor to the south.
Sadat condemned this action, saying that Egypt would

never accept a Communist country as its neighbor. The takeover plot was ultimately foiled, and the former Sudanese president was restored to power. But Sadat's hostile statements concerning the incident served to widen the gulf between him and the Soviets.

Toward the end of September, 1971, Sadat was invited to Moscow once more. Again he was promised arms and other military equipment. But nothing was ever delivered.

Meanwhile, United States Secretary of State William Rogers was stating that the United States would supply Israel with whatever weapons the country needed. He also announced that the United States and Israel had jointly begun to manufacture arms in Israel.

Sadat was back in Moscow early in 1972 in an effort to find out where his weapons were. He was running out of patience, and he let his anger show in meetings with the Soviets. Before he left, a Soviet official read a list of weapons that would be shipped to Egypt "forthwith."

Before any weapons arrived, Sadat received an urgent message from the Soviet leaders, asking him to pay another visit to Moscow. Sadat now realized that he was being used by the Soviets. A summit meeting between President Nixon and Russian Premier Brezhnev was in the planning stages. Before the Nixon–Brezhnev meeting took place, the Soviets wanted to demonstrate their firm position in the Middle East. A meeting with Sadat would accomplish that. Despite his disgust with the affair, Sadat accepted the invitation.

After Nixon's visit to Russia, a statement was issued jointly by Moscow and Washington calling for a military cooling-off period in the Middle East. The statement came as a shock to Sadat. "Military relaxation," to use the words of the statement, meant giving in to Israel.

Ultimately, Sadat ran out of patience. The weapons he wanted were never sent. All he received was a long message from the Soviet Union that analyzed the situation in the Middle East. It said nothing of the weapons that had been promised.

Sadat summoned the Soviet ambassador and told him that he rejected the message. That was only the beginning. He told him he wanted all Soviet military experts and their equipment out of Egypt within a week. Egypt's partnership with the Soviet Union was at an end.

In later years Sadat would cite this experience in explaining to the United States how it should deal with the Russians. When one moves to check the Soviet Union, it remains checked, Sadat believes. But allow the Soviets to infiltrate, and it will surely happen.

Pride, of course, was a major factor in Sadat's decision to boot the Russians out of Egypt. He wanted to tell the Russians that the destiny of Egypt was entirely in the hands of the Egyptian people.

Israel and the United States looked on with enormous interest. To diplomats of both countries, what Sadat had done was taken as a hopeful sign. Many of them interpreted it as meaning the Egyptians were no longer interested in fighting. Nothing could have been further from the truth.

The biggest problem of all facing Sadat was represented by those Israeli soldiers who had built shellproof concrete bunkers on the eastern bank of the Suez Canal. The fortifications were being called the Bar–Lev Line. Egyptian soldiers had dug in on the Canal's opposite bank. For a distance of over one hundred miles, the two sides kept constant watch on one another.

That the Israelis were still occupying the vast expanse of the Sinai rankled every Egyptian. Their presence was like an open wound that would not heal. To Sadat, the task of liberating the occupied territory was a sacred duty.

From a sand-bagged bunker, Sadat looks at Israeli positions on the occupied east bank of the Suez Canal in 1971.

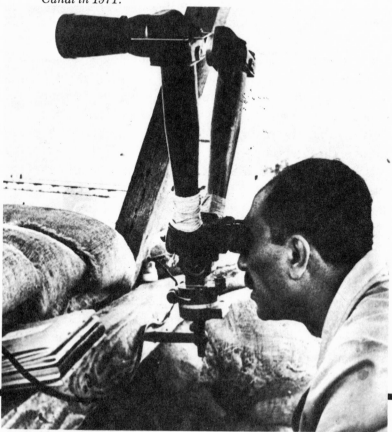

CHAPTER 7

THROUGHOUT THE EARLY YEARS OF his presidency, Sadat kept tensions at a high level by constantly announcing that war with Israel was just around the corner. He called 1971 "the year of decision." In December he was ready to launch a strike against Israel, but his plans were cancelled at the last minute. A crisis was developing between India and Pakistan that Sadat felt would overshadow any outbreak of war in the Middle East.

In the summer of 1972 he was prepared to move again. But that was the period in which he had ousted Russian personnel from Egypt. That had provided enough strain and tumult. Again he felt forced to postpone his operation.

All the while, Sadat explored every possible avenue in an attempt to achieve his goals by peaceful means. He prolonged a cease-fire arrangement with Israel that Nasser had accepted not long before his death. He approved a proposal by United Nations mediator Gunnar Jarring that Egypt acknowledge a state of peace with Israel in exchange for withdrawal from the Arab-occupied territories. He proposed an agreement whereby the Suez Canal would be cleared as the first step in a settlement with Israel. He sought an alliance with Syria and Libya that would serve to trigger the unification of the entire Arab world against Israel. He made appeal after appeal to the United Nations.

Nothing worked. The cease-fire agreement led nowhere. The Jarring proposal was rejected by the Israelis. The agreement to reopen the Canal proved unworkable when the Israelis refused to concede the principle of total withdrawal. About all that the Arab nations had in common was an inclination to disagree. The United Nations proved helpless.

Sadat also looked to the United States to pressure Israel into making concessions. It was, however, a presidential election year in the United States, with Richard Nixon opposing George McGovern. As might be the case with any American political figure, Nixon was aware of the importance of the Jewish vote in the United States. He realized that if he were to pressure Israel, it could be costly to him at the ballot box. Sadat was told to wait until after the election.

Sadat was in no mood for waiting. He had issued one threat after another, but he had not performed. His credibility was approaching an all-time low.

The election of 1972 came and went with Nixon winning decisively. Nothing happened. Sadat made one more attempt.

In February, 1973, he sent Hafiz Ismail—"my Kissinger," he called him—to see Nixon. The president welcomed him with open arms. He talked of finding a formula that would provide for Egyptian sovereignty in the Middle East and at the same time give the Israelis the assurance of security they demanded. Ismail left the White House in a buoyant mood. At last progress was being made.

Ismail was in Paris on his way home when he heard news that shocked him. Nixon had agreed to furnish Israel with almost one hundred new jet aircraft, thirty-six Skyhawks and forty-eight Phantoms.

To Sadat, that was the last straw. He was certain now that he could not negotiate with Richard Nixon. Every door he had opened had been slammed in his face. In March of that year Sadat decided to resume the war against Israel.

Sadat had no desire to destroy Israel or reconquer Palestine, nor did he even expect to regain for Egypt the greater part of the Sinai. Sadat's goals were largely political. He wanted to demonstrate to Israel that its military forces might not be quite as supreme as the nation's leaders believed. He wanted to puncture the feeling of security that the Israelis had.

The war was also meant to send a message to the United States. Make a choice, Sadat was saying to President Nixon. Do you want to put pressure on the Israelis, prevailing upon them to withdraw from the Sinai and other Arab lands? Or do you want a Middle East war and all the terrors that implies?

Early in 1973 Sadat appeared on Egyptian television and announced that "the stage of total confrontation" with Israel was about to begin. But by now no one believed him. He had cried wolf too often. Public opinion was beginning to turn against him. University students took to the streets of Cairo demanding action against Israel.

Sadat needed no urging. He quietly made preparations for the inevitable battle. He moved masterfully in lining up support, working out an arrangement with President Hafez al-Assad of Syria, in which it was agreed that they would wage war simultaneously. As Sadat attacked Israel from the west, al-Assad's forces would descend from the north.

During August of 1973, Sadat made a lightning visit to Riyadh in Saudi Arabia to tell King Faisal of his decision to go to war. One of the most powerful voices for conservatism in the Middle East, King Faisal had been a friend of Sadat's for more than two decades. The king voiced no strong objection to Sadat's plan, although he urged him to proceed with caution. In the past Faisal had bankrolled Arab governments battling Israel. He now agreed to do the same in Egypt's case, subsidizing Sadat's purchase of arms to the tune of $600 million. Lebanon, Morocco, Algeria, and Tunisia were other Arab countries that agreed to help.

To obtain the weapons he needed, Sadat resumed a dialogue with the Soviet Union. Through messages and trips to Moscow by Egyptian officials, he made it plain that in spite of his having expelled Soviet military experts from Egypt, he did not want to break diplomatic relations altogether. The result of his campaign was what Sadat described as the biggest arms deal ever. Almost overnight huge shipments of weapons began flooding into Egypt.

Of all the equipment Sadat purchased from the Soviets, a deadly new missile—the SAM-6 surface-to-air missile—was to prove the most devastating. From the first day of hostilities, it would take a heavy toll of American-made Phantom and Skyhawk jets. The Syrians were also furnished with SAM-6 missiles.

Called the Gainful, the SAM-6 was nineteen feet long and only six inches in diameter, solid fueled, and mounted on a tanklike vehicle. Unlike older SAM missiles, the SAM-6 could be moved along with armored forces, providing them with a protective cover that extended from treetop level to an altitude of 35,000 feet. The SAM-6 had a radar system in its warhead that guided it to its target at supersonic speed. Sadat was assured that while the Israelis knew how to defend themselves against earlier surface-to-air missiles, they had not yet developed methods to evade or neutralize the SAM-6; nor did they have a weapon that was its equal.

As the SAM-6 was destroying Israeli planes, the Egyptians had Soviet-built Snapper and Sagger antitank rockets to cope with Israel's armored forces. Both solid fueled, the Snapper and Sagger were accurate at distances of a mile or more. Each was directed by a gunner who simply lined up the target tank in a pair of cross hairs. Each missile was steered to its target by electronic signals transmitted through hair-thin wires that unspooled from the weapon as it flashed through the air.

For use as Egypt's main battle tanks, Sadat purchased hundreds of Soviet T-62s. Fitted with sixteen inches of armor plate, the 36.5-ton T-62 carried a 155mm cannon. Since the T-62 had never been used in combat before, the Israelis were unaware of its performance capabilities. Hundreds of older Soviet T-54 and T-55 tanks were other items in Egypt's armored supply kit.

Additional weapons in Sadat's arsenal included:

•The SAM-7 Strela, heat-seeking antiaircraft missiles that were fired in clusters of from eight to twelve rockets at a time. Unlike the older SAM missiles, the SAM-7 could be moved along with the armored force and fired in bunches from tracked vehicles or even individually by means of a single tube resting on an infantryman's shoulder.

• The SU-20, a swing-wing fighter plane designed specifically as a tank destroyer.

• The AS-5 Kelt, a winged, supersonic rocket with a range of 200 miles, to be fired from a bomber at a ground target.

• The Scud, a ground-to-ground missile with an eighty-mile range.

Israel, of course, had its own array of military equipment. Not only did the Israelis boast American-made jets, tanks, and artillery, plus missiles and rockets that the United States had developed during the Viet Nam war, it also had weapons of its own invention. Especially deadly were the American-made Sidewinder air-to-air heat-seeking missile; the Sparrow, an air-to-air missile that used radar to steer it to either a plane or tank target; and the Maverick, sometimes referred to as a "smart" bomb. Carried aboard a fighter-bomber, the Maverick had a small TV lens and computer in its nose. The pilot simply fixed a tank or missile emplacement in his sight and locked onto it. The TV camera then guided the bomb to its target.

Most sources agree that Sadat set D-Day for after Ramadan, the Muslim month of penance and fasting. That would mean the attack was to be launched during late October or early November.

But Sadat's plans were abruptly changed. On September 13, 1973, Israeli jets lured thirteen Syrian aircraft into an ambush over the Mediterranean Sea and shot every one of them down. President al-Assad of Syria immediately telephoned Sadat and expressed his fear that the Israelis might be on to their plans and were thinking of launching an assault of their own. Sadat and el-Assad then decided to attack in early October.

When Israeli intelligence reported that Egypt was building up its military strength along the Canal, the nation's military leaders merely shrugged. The Egyptians had been conducting such maneuvers for years. There was no indication that what they were now doing was anything different.

In Cairo everything was business as usual. There were no air raid drills, no evidence that war goods were being stockpiled.

Two weeks before the Egyptians were to strike, Sadat was host to two leaders of a Palestine guerrilla movement from Lebanon. He told them to prepare themselves, that Egypt was going to war. When the two men returned home, they reported Sadat's warning at an executive meeting of the Palestine Liberation Organization. The leaders chuckled, dismissing what Sadat had said as one more vain boast.

Sadat saw to it that the precise date of the attack remained a well-kept secret. He could not resist hinting at what was about to happen, however, in a speech late in September on the third anniversary of Nasser's death. Toward the end of the speech, in which he had been discussing problems on the home front, Sadat suddenly glanced skyward and said, "We know our goal and we are determined to attain it."

Not even Sadat's wife knew the exact date the attack was to be launched; although when he began having meeting after meeting with military leaders, she suspected that war was at hand. From bits and pieces of conversations with her husband, she was eventually able to figure out when it would begin. But she didn't feel she had the right to ask her husband to confirm her supposition. Besides she was afraid he might not answer or else tell her it was none of her business.

But Mrs. Sadat was worried about her children. The day before she was sure the war was to begin, she went to her husband and asked whether she should keep the children home from school the next day.

Sadat thought for a moment. "No," he said, "send them along, like all the others."

Then Mrs. Sadat said that she would like to keep a car out in front of the school, "just in case." Sadat agreed to that, but told his wife that she didn't have to bother until noontime. Mrs. Sadat then knew that the war was to begin around midday.

As his wife, Mrs. Sadat wanted to encourage her husband; but she realized that he did not need any encouragement. He was quietly confident about what the days ahead would bring. Not everyone shared Sadat's positive feelings. Early in October, Sadat met with the Soviet ambassador and told him that Egypt and Syria were soon to begin military operations against Israel. He asked the ambassador what the Soviet attitude would be. The ambassador didn't answer the question right away. But the next day he called Sadat to tell him he wanted to see him on an extremely urgent matter. At the meeting the ambassador explained the Soviet leaders wanted to be granted permission to fly four huge transport planes to Cairo to carry Soviet civilians back to Russia. The planes would be arriving the next day.

Sadat was dumbfounded. With war about to break

out, the Soviets were fleeing the country. It was not a vote of confidence.

Early in the afternoon of October 6, the Day of Atonement, Yom Kippur, the most solemn day in the Jewish religious year, the Egyptian army launched a massive assault on a broad front across the Suez Canal and into the Sinai. So did the Syrian army. The Syrians were soon stopped. The Egyptians were not.

In the 1967 war Egypt had sent waves of infantrymen and armor into battle only to see them pulverized by Israeli air power. This time it was different. Using Russian artillery and surface-to-air missiles, the Egyptians created an umbrella of protection for their troops.

Up and down the 103-mile length of the Canal Egyptian forces in small assault boats quickly erected bridges. Some were old-fashioned pontoon bridges, formed by lashing boats side-by-side to support a roadway. Others were more modern, laid down by Soviet-built amphibious vehicles that deposited ladderlike bridge sections as they chugged across the Canal. Where no bridges were erected, soldiers made their way across in small boats and rafts.

To deceive the Israeli forces, some Egyptian soldiers had bathed in the Canal shortly before the attack. One Israeli radioman reported back to a secondary defense line that hundreds of thousands of Egyptians were swimming toward their fort. They pleaded for reinforcements.

With the troops went the Soviet-built tanks, not only the huge T-62s but the smaller T-54s as well. The Egyptians swept over Israel's Bar–Lev Line and pushed out into the desert, as the Israeli forces fell back. Then, by the tens of thousands, the Egyptians began fanning out along the waterway, penetrating to positions as deep as twelve miles inside the Sinai, just far enough to remain under the protection of their surface-to-air missiles.

At the same time some two hundred Egyptian supersonic jets were bombing targets in Israel—air defense centers, aerial combat headquarters, electronic warfare installations, and gun and missile emplacements. Egyptian commando units were assigned to work their way behind Israeli lines and disrupt supply routes.

Sadat directed fighting from an office at army headquarters on the outskirts of Cairo. He observed the strict Ramadan fast. Most days he napped for two hours in the afternoon, then worked late into the night, holding meetings with top staff members. He listened attentively to his generals, respecting their knowledge; but he made the important decisions himself.

By the end of the first week the Egyptians had managed to put approximately one hundred thousand men and a thousand tanks on the east bank of the Canal. The Egyptian flag was flying in the Sinai once again.

While the Egyptians were strengthening their 103-mile long bridgehead, the Israelis focused their attention on the Syrian battlefield some 300 miles away. There the Israelis launched their first major counterattack of the war, lashing into the Syrian forces. At first the Syrians fell back; but then their resistance stiffened, and eventually *they* counterattacked, forcing the Israelis to withdraw.

By this time other Arab countries were hurrying to the support of Syria and Egypt. Kuwait sent a small detachment of troops to the Suez Canal area. Saudi Arabia and Tunisia each contributed about one thousand men. Iraq did more, moving more than eighteen thousand infantry-men and tanks to the Syrian front.

The Jordan joined in. Like Egypt and Syria, Jordan shared a border with Israel and thus posed a particular threat to the Israelis. King Hussein ordered elements of the small but highly professional Jordanian army to help out the Syrians.

Although the outcome of the war was still in doubt, one thing was clear: The Arabs had never fought better against the Israelis. As a result, Arabs around the world had their pride restored. The world would no longer laugh when Arab armies threatened to fight.

Wilton Wynn, a correspondent for *Time* magazine, re-called being driven across the Canal in the first weeks of the war and seeing Egyptian troops standing on their tanks as he passed by, calling out, *"Allahu Akbara"* ("God is the greatest"). Other troops gave a clasped-

Posters hailing Sadat decorate a Cairo coffee shop not long after the beginning of the 1973 war with Israel.

hands salute of welcome or flashed V-for-Victory signs with their fingers. Everywhere he went, Wynn found Egyptian soldiers in buoyant spirits and bursting with confidence, behaving as if the war was over and they had won it.

On the eleventh day of the war, Sadat scheduled an address to the Egyptian People's Assembly. As he drove to the Parliament Building, tens of thousands of Egyptians lined the streets of Cairo to cheer. "Victory for Sadat!" they chanted. "Victory for Sadat!"

In his address, Sadat talked of his aims in war and peace, but also celebrated the dawn of a new era for Egypt and the Arab world. "The Egyptian armed forces performed a miracle, by any military standards," he said. "The risk was enormous and the sacrifices were grave. But the results of the first six-hour battle of our war were magnificent. Our wounded nation has restored its honor, and the political map of the Middle East has been changed."

In what he called an "open letter" to President Nixon, Sadat offered a set of peace proposals. They included a cease-fire, provided that the Israelis would, under international supervision, withdraw from the territories they now occupied; an international peace conference at the United Nations to be attended by Palestinian as well as Arab leaders; and a promise to reopen the Suez Canal, still plugged with wreckage from the Six-Day War, as soon as the Israeli withdrawal had been completed.

The speech was notable for its calmness and reason. Obviously Sadat now felt strong enough to talk about peace and the other objectives he was seeking. Before

October 6 and the crossing of the Egyptian forces into the Sinai, he could not have done so.

The people of Cairo were jubilant. Newspapers called Sadat's address a "triumph of reason" and "the most beautiful speech ever delivered by an Arab head of state to the present generation."

CHAPTER

8

EVEN AS SADAT WAS ADDRESSING the Egyptian People's Assembly, setting forth his goals in war and peace, Egyptian and Israeli forces were locked in one of the biggest tank battles in history. By some estimates more tanks and armor were involved than in the classic tank battle between the Germans and British at El Alamein in 1942.

Israeli forces had discovered a weak spot between two Egyptian armies and had begun driving a wedge of armor and infantrymen between them. The Egyptians were slow to react to the thrust. By the time they began to throw up resistance, it was too late. The Israelis had crossed over the Canal, fanning out to establish a ten- to twenty-mile-wide beachhead near the town of Deversoir between Suez and Ismailia. Hundreds of Israeli tanks went pouring into the pocket. From this foothold the Israelis were able to disrupt Egypt's lines of supply and communication, and attack missle installations.

Sadat reacted coolly. He ordered the bridgehead surrounded by a wall of rockets and ringed by tanks. He had recently received 150 tanks from President Houari Boumedienne of Algeria and another 140 from Marshal Tito of Yugoslavia. The Yugoslavian tanks had arrived loaded with fuel and ammunition and were sent into action immediately. Sadat looked upon the Israeli troops within the west bank bridgehead as his prisoners. Their presence there meant their doom.

As the fighting became more intense and the United States began launching a massive effort to resupply the Israelis, the Arab countries introduced a new weapon—a weapon they had been threatening to use for years—a cutback on shipments of oil to the United States and other countries helping Israel. The United States was already struggling with an energy problem. Suddenly it became much worse. "NO GAS" signs began appearing at American gasoline stations.

What Sadat had done, through skillful negotiation and with the active support of King Faisal of Saudi Arabia, was to prevail upon the petroleum-exporting nations to use oil as a political weapon. He was impressing upon the United States the need for adopting policies more favorable to Egypt and the Arab world.

Meanwhile, frantic diplomatic efforts were being made to impose a cease-fire upon the warring armies. The United States and the Soviet Union were determined to put an end to the fighting—and eventually did. On October 22 the United States and the Soviet Union called for a meeting of the United Nations Security Council and co-sponsored a resolution calling for an immediate end to hostilities. Both Egypt and Israel accepted the resolution.

Under its terms the battle lines of October 22 were to be regarded as the cease-fire lines. But two hours after the cease-fire order was issued, Sadat claims that Israel launched two attacks designed to extend the territory held by its forces. One Israeli armored column struck out for Suez, the other for Ismailia. Once Sadat realized what was happening, he ordered his army commanders to resist the Israelis' advance. Israel's plan, according to Sadat, was to attempt to intimidate the Egyptians and improve its bargaining position during the peace talks that were to come.

While the Israeli forces were deterred in their attempt to seize Ismailia, they managed to reach the outskirts of Suez. By that time Sadat was in touch with American and Soviet officials in an effort to get them to restrain the Israelis. He explained that he would be willing to have American and Soviet troops land on Egyptian territory to insure that the Israeli forces pulled back to the battle lines of October 22.

Soon thereafter United States Secretary of State Henry Kissinger arrived in Cairo to meet with Sadat. He asked Sadat what he wanted. Sadat explained that he wanted Israeli forces to withdraw to the battle lines of October 22, the date of the cease-fire agreement. The two men discussed the bridgehead the Israelis had established on the west bank of the Nile. Sadat pointed out that he had 800 tanks surrounding the Israeli forces and their 400 tanks. Were Sadat to order an attack on the Israeli pocket, he was certain a blood bath would take place.

But it never occurred. Largely through the efforts of Henry Kissinger, an agreement that provided for a two-stage disengagement of forces was hammered out. Sadat liked Kissinger. They had no difficulty in understanding each other's objectives. In dealing with the American Secretary of State, Sadat said he was looking at the "real face" of the United States, the face he had long wanted to see.

The agreement was signed by Egyptian and Israeli officers at a ceremony on November 11 at Kilometer 101 on the Cairo–Suez road. The two warring nations were at long last in direct diplomatic contact.

Despite the presence of the Israeli forces on the east bank of the Nile, Sadat's acceptance of the cease-fire proposal was deeply resented by the Egyptian army and the people. They believed that they had had the Israelis on the run. The Egyptian army had not been dealt any crippling blows. The country's air force was largely intact.

Sadat, however, had no reason to continue the fighting. He had accomplished what he had set out to do. From the first day he had become president of Egypt, Sadat's ambition had been to dislodge the Israelis from the territory they had seized in the Six-Day War. He had now achieved that goal. Under the terms of the cease-fire agreement, the bulk of the Israeli forces was to withdraw to positions that were twenty-two miles east of the Suez Canal. An important first step had been taken. The many thousands of square miles of Sinai territory still under Israeli control would be the subject of future negotiations.

Sadat referred to Henry Kissinger as "one of my most intimate friends." Here the two men hold a press conference in Alexandria in 1975.

The cease-fire agreement was also significant because it marked an end to Sadat's relationship with the Soviet Union. In the early days of the war, the Soviets had demanded that Egypt accept a cease-fire along the then-existing battle lines. Premier Aleksei Kosygin had even gone to Cairo to urge Sadat to accept this course of action.

Sadat rejected the Soviet plan. It would solve nothing. He wanted the Israeli forces eventually to give up *all* the territory they occupied in the Sinai, and this was not provided for in the Soviet proposal. Sadat and Kosygin argued heatedly.

It was bad enough that Sadat had turned his back on the Soviets. Then to accept a settlement negotiated by the United States Secretary of State was even worse. Indeed it was the breaking point. Sadat's friendship with the Soviets was at an end. At the same time he agreed to resume diplomatic relations with the United States.

Another result of the war and the cease-fire was the enormous increase in prestige that Sadat enjoyed. This was apparent in his stepped-up popularity and support at home. Among world leaders there was new respect for Sadat's shrewdness, for the diplomatic skills he had displayed in getting the Arab nations to work together toward a common goal.

What Sadat had done was to give the Arabs their first taste of victory over Israel in twenty-five years. In doing so he had shattered the twin myths of Israeli invincibility and of Arab incompetence. He had done much to wipe away the deep feeling of inferiority that had cloaked an entire generation of Arabs. It did not matter that Sadat's victories were short-lived and limited in size. They were victories. They gave the Arab world a new sense of self-respect and dignity.

The successes were not achieved without a heavy cost. While Sadat has never revealed the number of casualties suffered by the Egyptians, it has been said unofficially that more than six thousand men died. Perhaps an equal number of Israelis died.

Sadat himself suffered a painful loss. His twenty-four-year-old half-brother Atif, a fighter pilot, was killed in the first hour of the war. 'Atif, whom Sadat had raised, was as close to him as a son.

In history books, Sadat's war has several different names. Some call it the Yom Kippur War or the War of the Day of Judgment. To others, it is the October War. It depends upon one's political leanings. Others, to avoid any political commitment, call it simply the fourth Arab–Israeli War. Whatever name it bears, there is no denying its importance. Edward R. F. Sheehan, writing in *The New York Times*, ranked the war and its effects on a par with the Arab conquests of the Middle Ages and with the birth of Arab and Egyptian nationalism, calling it one of the most significant events in Arab history.

Once the cease-fire agreement had been signed and the warring parties had complied with its terms, the next step would be to negotiate a peace settlement. The Arabs and Israelis were clear in what each wanted. The Arab nations wanted Israeli forces to withdraw from the territories they had overrun in the 1967 war and had occupied since. This amounted to six times as much land as Israel controlled in 1948.

What Israel wanted out of the settlement was the right

to live in peace within secure and recognized boundaries, plus an admission by the Arab states of Israel's right to exist as a nation.

Besides these overall problems, there were several trouble spots, including:

•The Sinai—Sadat wanted this huge expanse of desert returned to Egyptian control. Israel had no strong objection to withdrawing from the Sinai, providing the border between the Sinai and Israel would be demilitarized. In other words, Israel wanted security against future attacks across the border.

One solution called for creating a zone twenty to thirty miles wide at the border—wide enough to keep each side out of artillery or short-range rocket attack from the other. A permanent United Nations force would occupy the border zone.

•The Golan Heights—Israel wanted similar guarantees that Syrian forces would never again launch an attack over this disputed stretch of rocky terrain. A multinational peace-keeping force was proposed as a solution.

•The West Bank of the River Jordan—Since this intruded into the very heart of Israel, any discussions concerning it were charged with emotion. King Hussein of Jordan once suggested that the problem of the West Bank settlements might be solved by creating a demilitarized Palestinian state on the West Bank. While the territory might be administered by Jordan, there would be United Nations observers posted there. The borders of this zone would be open to the Israelis so that they, too, could keep an eye on things.

The city of Jerusalem was a particular problem. Although the Israelis had allowed the Muslims freedom to visit their holy places in Jerusalem in the months before the war, Israel's occupation of the Old City, where the religious shrines were located, outraged the Arab world.

One proposed compromise suggested that the Israelis would retain control in all Jewish sections of the city, while Arabs would administer the Arab sections. The city's common services would be administered by a joint planning board. All religious faiths would be guaranteed the right to visit the city's sacred shrines.

•The Palestinian refugees—These Arab people, as many as four million of them by some estimates, loomed as one of the major obstacles to peace. Many of them had fled or had been forced from their land when the state of Israel had been created some twenty-eight years before. They claimed the land of Israel as their birthright.

Sadat, in fact, called the Palestinian refugees the "whole core" of the peace problem. He said peace would never be realized until it was solved. Sadat called for the creation of a Palestinian state on the West Bank and the Gaza Strip with a corridor between them, and an agreement upon the relation between this state and Jordan, according to what the two parties—the Palestinians and the Jordanians—agreed upon.

Increasingly, the world was being kept aware of the problem of the Palestinian refugees through the efforts of the guerrilla group known as the Palestine Liberation Organization—the PLO. Organized by the Arab heads of state in 1964 to liberate Palestine from Israeli control, the PLO, by the early 1970s was seeking to achieve its goals by terrorist activities. In 1973 alone the organization claimed responsibility for 1,251 "military operations" inside Israeli-held territory. The following year, 1974, the chairman of the PLO, Yasir Arafat, appeared before the United Nations General Assembly in New York and won U. N. support for the right of the Palestinians to independence and sovereignty.

Concerning the Palestinian issue, there was a general agreement that there would be no easy solution. Indeed, a decade later the problem would still be serving as one of the chief barriers to a permanent peace.

CHAPTER 9

IN OCTOBER, 1973, LESS THAN THREE weeks after he had ordered his tanks across the Nile and into the Sinai, Sadat met with a construction engineer, his friend Osman Ahmed Osman. Sadat explained that he wanted Osman to prepare plans for reconstructing the cities along the Suez Canal that had been devastated during the war, explaining that he wanted to rebuild the towns right in the range of Israeli guns. He wanted to show the Israelis he didn't intend to make war on them again.

Aside from military activity, there had been little life in the area. The city of Suez, at the southern terminus of the Canal, once home to more than a quarter-million people, now had a population of ten thousand. In Ismailia, a city of one hundred thousand located about midway between the northern and southern ends of the Canal, virtually every building had been either damaged or destroyed by bombs, missiles, or artillery fire.

Sadat also gambled that he could open the Canal again and keep it open, despite the fact it would be vulnerable to easy attack. The need for the waterway had never been greater. The Canal reduced the travel time of ships bound for Marseilles from the Persian Gulf by 50 percent, and to east coast ports of the United States by 27 percent. Some economists were saying that the closure of the Canal was costing consumers as much as $10 billion a year in the extra expense involved in hauling petroleum and other goods around Africa's southern tip.

The Canal had special importance to Egypt, of course. In 1966, the last full year in which it operated, the Canal produced tolls that amounted to $200 million. Egypt's Suez Canal Authority planned to deepen the Canal from thirty-eight to forty feet so that larger ships could be handled. Once such plans were carried out, the Canal might bring Egypt as much as $1 billion a year.

The United States played an important role in the reopening of the Canal. During the negotiations that followed the October War, Sadat happened to mention to Henry Kissinger that he was seeking assistance in getting the Canal cleared.

Kissinger was eager to do what he could. "Give me an hour," he said. Kissenger then called the White House and the Pentagon. He returned to Sadat with a question: "Would you allow the U. S. helicopter-carrier *Iwo Jima*, which has on board clearing equipment, to anchor at Port Said and start helping you?"

Such a suggestion would have been unthinkable only a year or so before. And even at the time there were American diplomats who voiced fears that Egyptian coast artillery batteries might fire upon the *Iwo Jima*. But Sadat gladly accepted Kissinger's offer, knowing that no such incident would occur. Two days later the *Iwo Jima* steamed into the harbor at Port Said to be warmly greeted by units of the Egyptian navy. Almost immediately helicopters from the carrier began towing minesweeping sleds over the length of the waterway, searching for magnetic mines.

By June, 1975, the work had been completed. The Egyptians spent almost $300 million in the clearing effort. As Sadat was being driven to the ceremonies that were to mark the reopening of the waterway, a man suddenly appeared on the roadway ahead of his limousine. The man was waving his arms frantically. Sadat's driver stopped. The man was elderly, with long white hair that fell over his shoulders. He was dressed in a long white robe and leather sandals. His face was solemn.

Guards sprang from cars that had been accompanying Sadat, seized the man, and began wrestling him toward the side of the road. Sadat ordered his men to stop.

The man stared at Sadat, then suddenly fell to his knees and began to pray. It was a prayer of thanksgiving to God. When he was finished, the man rose to his feet and signaled Sadat's motorcade to continue its journey. Then he disappeared into the crowd.

For eight years the Canal people had lived as evacuees. Now this man and the others like him were back in their homeland. That afternoon, dressed in a white admiral's uniform, Sadat boarded a destroyer and sailed through the Canal, officially reopening it. But the memory of the man who had stopped his car to express his gratitude gripped Sadat throughout the day.

Opening the Canal was done at considerable risk. The Canal itself and the three principal Canal towns—Port Said, Suez, and Ismailia—were within easy range of Israeli artillery. Whether Israel would ever use those guns depended upon the outcome of the peace negotiations. And the peace negotiations were not going well. It became obvious that the longer the disputed points went unresolved, the greater was the likelihood of a fifth Arab–Israeli war.

In the weeks immediately following the October War, Sadat had been optimistic, believing that peace would come quickly thanks to the support of the United States. The first disengagement-of-forces agreement took less than two weeks to complete.

But late in 1974, when Henry Kissinger sought to negotiate the second disengagement-of-forces agreement, he encountered one roadblock after another. Washington was gripped by the Watergate affair. President Nixon's authority had collapsed. President Gerald Ford, who assumed office in August, 1974, being a nonelected president, was regarded as weak by the Israelis. Kissinger's efforts for peace were thus paralyzed.

Another problem came from the divided government of Israeli Premier Yitzhak Rabin. Rabin was not secure enough or bold enough to make concessions to Sadat.

Sadat wanted the Abu Rudeis oil fields, located in the Sinai, returned to Egyptian control. They had been pumping oil for Israel since they had been captured in the Six-Day War in 1967.

The same week that Sadat reopened the Suez Canal he met with President Ford in Salzburg, Austria. The meeting led to a new effort that eventually restored the western edge of the Sinai and the Abu Rudeis oil fields to Egypt's control.

Sadat, however, was looking for more than a step-by-step solution to the problems in the Middle East. He wanted a comprehensive settlement that would end the climate of strife that had prevailed for more than thirty years.

Shortly after Jimmy Carter's election to the presidency in 1976, Sadat went to Washington D. C. to meet with him. Carter and Sadat reviewed peace strategy together. Sadat felt comfortable with Carter. He found him to be honest with himself and honest in dealing with others. He felt he was dealing with a man who understood what he, Sadat, wanted. He considered Carter a man of religious faith and high principles—"a farmer like me," Sadat said.

Meanwhile, Sadat was experiencing troubles at home. In mid-January bloody riots broke out in Cairo and Alexandria to protest spiraling food prices and the government's general failure to raise living standards. More than eighty Egyptians were killed and nearly one thousand were arrested. The army had to be called in to restore order.

President Sadat meets with President Gerald Ford in 1975.

The Russians were causing problems, too. Sadat believed that they might have had a hand in the January riots. It also bothered him that the Russians were installing sophisticated electronic listening devices in Libya. When Sadat was unable to get the Russians to put a halt to such activities through diplomatic channels, he ordered the Egyptian air force to destroy the bases. He felt he could not worry about *all* his borders at once.

In October, 1977, the United States and the Soviet Union issued a joint statement on peace in the Middle East. It mentioned "the legitimate rights" of the Palestinians. American Jewish organizations and various pro-Israeli groups reacted bitterly to the declaration. In a subsequent bargaining session with Israel's Moshe Dayan, Carter backed down, saying that the U. S. / Soviet declaration would not be used as a basis for future peace talks.

Sadat now knew that he could not depend wholly on the United States in forming a peace strategy. He would have to pursue other channels.

Another problem was bearing down on him. Israel had built up an enormous arsenal of modern arms, including nuclear weapons; but as the military strength of Israel had been growing, that of Egypt had been on the decline. With relations with the Soviets at a low ebb, Egypt could no longer call upon them for weapons. Sadat's military commanders told him that if war broke out, Egyptian forces would be smashed.

In September, 1977, Sadat received a personal letter from President Carter. The letter was handwritten and sealed with wax. Since the letter was of a personal nature, Sadat has never revealed its contents, only to say that it included an up-to-date review of the situation in the Middle East.

In replying to the president, Sadat suggested some bold action. But at the same time he had no idea what form that action might take. With the exchange of letters, Sadat began a fresh appraisal of the situation. He realized that there was a tremendous psychological barrier standing in the way of any peace effort between Egypt and Israel, a barrier of suspicion, fear, hate, and misunderstanding.

Because of the wall, neither side was willing to believe the other. And both were quite unprepared to accept any message transmitted through United States officials.

It was at this stage that Sadat called upon the inner strengths he had developed in Cell 54 of the Cairo Central Prison many years before, strengths that expanded his capacity for change.

As Sadat had pointed out in his book, an individual who cannot change the fabric of his thought will never be able to change reality or go forward. Sadat realized that in order to put forward any bold approach toward achieving peace, he would have to revise his own way of regarding Israel. No change would ever occur until a change in ideas had taken place.

Sadat was pondering the situation when he learned that his friend Nicolae Ceausescu, president of Rumania, had recently met with Menahem Begin, the new premier of Israel. Begin was a man with a hawkish image. When he had been elected premier of Israel, even Jimmy Carter had suggested it might be a backward step. Sadat invited himself to Rumania to discuss Begin with Ceausescu.

Ceausescu assured Sadat that Begin wanted a peaceful solution. He described the Israeli leader as a strong man and one who would use that strength to work on behalf of peace. Sadat knew that Ceausescu had maintained a close relationship with the Israelis. Moreover, he trusted Ceausescu's judgment.

Sadat's first idea was to call a conference of the world's superpowers to meet with the representatives of Middle East countries. But he rejected that plan. Instead of hiding behind the big powers, he decided to take matters into his own hands, to face the Israelis on their own ground.

And so it was that Sadat, in November, 1977, was led to his "bold action," a change in behavior so drastic that no one believed him when he announced what he was planning to do. In a speech to the Egyptian Parliament early in the month, Sadat declared, "There is no time to lose. I am ready to go to the ends of the earth if that will save one of my soldiers, one of my officers, from being scratched. I am ready to go to their house, to the Knesset [the Israeli Parliament], to discuss peace with the Israeli leaders."

Almost everyone believed that Sadat was speaking figuratively. It was uniform policy among Arab nations never to deal publicly with Israeli officials. No one was expecting Sadat to deviate from a policy that was so deeply ingrained in Arab custom. Arab leaders would not even sit at the negotiating table with their Zionist counterparts. And later, after the creation of Israel, the policy hardened. At an Arab–Israel conference in Lausanne, Switzerland, in 1949, the two sides stayed in separate hotels and communicated only through messengers.

Not long after his speech to the Egyptian Parliament, the United States ambassador called on Sadat and handed him a formal invitation from Israel Premier Menahem Begin to come to Jerusalem. Sadat would call his journey a "sacred mission." The course of events in the Middle East were about to be changed.

From the moment of his historic flight from an air base in the Suez Canal Zone to Tel Aviv's Ben Gurion Airport, Sadat's image was carried by television satellites to viewers around the world. He stepped out of the plane to be greeted by Menahem Begin and stood at attention next to Begin as an Israeli military band played first the Egyp-

Sadat greets Alfred Atherton, U.S. Ambassador to Egypt, in Cairo.

tian national anthem, *By God of Old, Who is My Weapon*, and then the Israeli *Hatikvah*. Next, with Begin at his side, Sadat walked along the receiving line, greeting those who had once been among his most determined enemies—former premiers Yitzhak Rabin and Golda Meir; foreign minister Moshe Dayan, whose forces Sadat had battled in 1973; and General Ariel Sharon, who had led the Israel counterattack in the October War. Sadat joked with Sharon. "If you attempt to cross the West Bank again," he said, "I'll put you in jail."

"Oh, no!" said Sharon with a grin. "I'm Minister of Culture now."

Then Sadat spotted Mordechai Gur, Israel's Chief of Staff. Gur had warned that Sadat's visit was a trick meant to mask a surprise military attack. Sadat explained to Gur that he was not one to practice ethical deception. Strategic deception, perhaps, or tactical deception. But ethical deception? Never.

Early the next day, fulfilling a vow he had made to himself, Sadat prayed at the al-Aqsa Mosque in the Old City of Jerusalem, one of the Muslim world's holiest places.

Sadat went to the Knesset, the Israeli Parliament, in the afternoon and made his speech. He made certain demands upon Israel, calling for the return to Arab sovereignty of all the territory Israeli forces had conquered during the Six-Day War in 1967. He also championed the cause of the Palestinian people and their right to determine their own future, including the right to establish their own state.

But Sadat also had words of compassion for the Israelis. "We used to reject you, true," he said. "We refused to meet you anywhere, true. We referred to you as the 'so-called' Israel, true. At international conferences our representatives refused to exchange greetings with you, true. At the 1973 Geneva Peace Conference our delegates did not exchange a single direct word with you, true. Yet today we agree to live with you in permanent peace and justice. Israel has become an accomplished fact recognized by the whole world and the superpowers. We welcome you to live among us in peace and security."

Sadat had been tough in his speech, making it clear that there would be no more war, but only on condition that Israel accepted a peace agreement that included a return of all Arab territories. But he had been compassionate, too, wholeheartedly acknowledging Israel's right to exist. Not since the founding of Israel in 1948 had the will for peace been so strong.

In his historic trip to Jerusalem in 1977, Sadat prayed at the Al-Aqsa Mosque in the Old City, one of the Muslim world's holiest places.

CHAPTER 10

WHEN SADAT RETURNED TO CAIRO, he was given a hero's welcome. Hundreds of thousands of Egyptians lined the streets to cheer and applaud him. But in other Arab capitals his journey to Jerusalem set off storms of criticism. Syria's President Hafez al-Assad declared that November 19, the day of Sadat's arrival in Jerusalem, should be deemed a national day of mourning. *"Sadat Went to Lick Zionists' Boots,"* screamed a headline in a Syrian newspaper. In Libya the often-hysterical Muammar al-Qaddafi closed the country's airports and docks to Egyptian traffic. In Saudi Arabia there were angry charges that Sadat had broken what had been a unified Arab front.

Many Israelis, while saluting Sadat for his courage in opening a new phase in Arab–Israeli relations, were not cheered by the contents of his speech. They said his terms for a peace settlement were really no different from earlier Arab demands—an Israeli withdrawal to the 1967 borders and a Palestinian state.

Nevertheless, in the weeks following Sadat's Jerusalem visit, a momentum for peace was apparent. Then Sadat and Israeli Prime Minister Menahem Begin met in Ismailia late in December, 1977. The meeting was a disappointment. Sadat ordered the Egyptian delegation to leave, saying there was absolutely no hope for reaching an agreement. Later, he would brand Begin an "obstacle to peace."

A major stumbling block was the West Bank question. Sadat wanted the Israelis to give up the West Bank territories, even if they were to do it at some future date. Begin made it clear that he intended Israeli military forces to remain on the West Bank indefinitely.

Through the early months of 1978, the situation did not change. It was then that President Jimmy Carter and Secretary of State Cyrus Vance began to play a bigger role in the negotiations, seeking to keep alive the momentum for peace that had been triggered by Sadat. The involvement of the United States eventually led to a summit meeting between Sadat and Begin, with Carter directly involved. Camp David, the presidential retreat in the Catoctin Mountains of Maryland, about seventy miles from Washington, was the scene of the meeting.

The Camp David conference, although it began in an

Sadat is greeted by Secretary of State Cyrus Vance, 1979.

(OFFICIAL PHOTO, THE WHITE HOUSE)

atmosphere of gloom, provided results beyond the greatest hopes of the three participating leaders. Israel conceded the fundamental principle that the Sinai belongs to Egypt. The Sinai border established in 1906 was acknowledged as the permanent legal border. Israel agreed to remove its military forces and settlers from the Sinai.

Israel also agreed to the construction of a highway between the Sinai and Jordan, crossing Israeli territory near Eilat, with guaranteed free and peaceful passage between Egypt and Jordan. The highway thus provided the long-sought land link between North Africa and the Arabian Peninsula, parts of the Arab world physically divided by Israel's presence.

At Camp David with President Jimmy Carter and Prime Minister Menahem Begin.

In another concession Israel gave up oil fields the country had developed in the Sinai. These were providing about one-quarter of Israel's total petroleum requirements. The United States promised that should Israel run short of oil at any time over the ensuing fifteen years, it would make up the difference.

Israel's three major airfields in the Sinai were to be replaced by two new ones in the Negev Desert. The construction of these new airfields was to be financed by the United States. It was estimated that it would cost from $1 billion to $3 billion to make them operational.

This was not the only financial commitment made by the United States. Both Egypt and Israel were each to receive about $2 billion more for military aid and $500 mil-

Sadat with President Carter during the Camp David meetings.

lion more for economic support. At the time Egypt was receiving from the United States about $800 million a year in economic aid; Israel, about $1.8 billion.

Sadat's concessions included full recognition and acceptance of Israel. Egypt would end its economic boycott and grant Israeli ships the right to use the Suez Canal. Israel would also be permitted to buy oil from the Sinai fields returned to Egypt.

Sadat also agreed to the demiliterization of the Sinai and to limit the Egyptian armed forces in the area to one division. The United Nations would be asked to station troops along the Sinai's eastern border, or a multinational force would be created for that purpose.

In the midst of the negotiations, Sadat and Begin were awarded the Nobel Peace Prize for their efforts toward the settlement of the Arab–Israeli conflict. Sadat was hailed by the Nobel committee for his precedent-setting visit to Jerusalem, which was described as opening a break in the "psychological wall" that had separated the two countries.

Sadat meets with Carter at the White House in 1979.

Many critical problems were not settled by what came to be called the Camp David Accords. The settlement of the West Bank Palestinians was one such problem. Sadat and Begin were in no position to solve that problem alone. Any solution required the participation of Jordan and the Palestinians themselves. The future of the Gaza Strip and of the Golan Heights were other matters the Camp David talks left open.

At ceremonies at the White House in March, 1979, Sadat and Begin signed, and President Carter witnessed, two documents—one that outlined a framework for a comprehensive settlement of the Middle East conflict and another that set a framework for an Egyptian–Israeli peace treaty.

At the signing ceremonies, Sadat called the documents ". . . a historic turning point of great significance for all peace-loving nations. . . Today a new dawn is emerging from the darkness of the past." He paid tribute to President Carter and the role he had played.

Sadat also acknowledged that problems lay ahead.

The signing of the Camp David Accords, March 26, 1979.

"The signing of these documents mark only the beginning of peace," he stated. "Other steps remain to be taken without delay."

Sadat returned to Cairo to receive a tumultuous welcome. But even as he was accepting the cheers, the Arab countries were plotting their revenge on Egypt. In some parts of the Arab world, what Sadat had signed was being called a traitor's treaty. Even moderate Arab states warned that the treaty could never be successful because it did not solve the Palestinian problem.

The Arab leaders did more than merely condemn the treaty. They took concrete action, breaking diplomatic

Page 7 of the Camp David Accords as signed by President Sadat and Prime Minister Begin, and witnessed by President Carter.

relations with Egypt and instituting an economic boycott of the country. The headquarters of the Arab League was moved from Cairo to Tunis.

Sadat was deeply hurt by the action taken by his Arab brothers. He once described this period as very painful, but he would not back down on the commitments he had made.

The PLO launched a campaign of terror to protest the treaty. There were sabotage attempts against Israeli and Egyptian embassies in Cyprus and Turkey. A bomb exploded at the airport in Frankfort, Germany, in a package bound for an Israeli school.

But Sadat pushed ahead, continuing to negotiate with Begin on the subject of the future of the Palestinians. There was general agreement that the Palestinians be granted "autonomy," that they be granted their independence, that they have the right of self-government. That is the dictionary definition of autonomy. But Sadat and Begin each attached a different meaning to the word. As one United States diplomatic official put it, "For Sadat, autonomy is a millimeter or so short of full sovereignty.

Congratulations are offered after the signing of the Accords.

(OFFICIAL PHOTO, THE WHITE HOUSE)

For Begin, it is barely a millimeter beyond what exists now."

At length, Sadat became resigned to the fact that the differences that existed between himself and Begin might never be resolved. Begin did not help the situation by encouraging the settling of Jews in West Bank territories in an effort to bolster Israeli claims there. Sadat called the policy selfish, claiming that more than 90 percent of the Israeli people wanted peace. "But the government? I don't know," he said.

With the peace process bogged down, Sadat turned his attention to the domestic problems of his country. He was sixty-one now, completing his eleventh year as Egypt's president (he had been nominated and affirmed for a

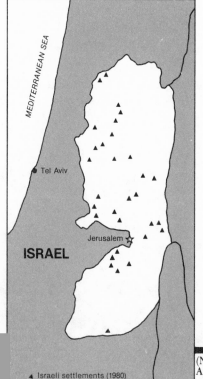

Israel's West Bank settlements, 1980.

(Neil Katine, Herb Field Art Studio)

second six-year term in 1976). Yet many of the problems he faced at home were the same as those that had confronted him when he first took office—limited land available for cultivation, a government swollen with unproductive workers, frightful unemployment, and an illiteracy rate of about 75 percent. A woman shopper in Cairo, quoted by *The New York Times*, summed up the feelings of many when she said: "Sadat is very smart in his international moves, but I do not think he really understands the sufferings of the Egyptian people."

Many of these sufferings spring from the country's high rate of population growth, estimated to be between 2 and 3 percent a year. Egypt's population, which about doubled in the period from 1952 to 1978, when it reached forty million, could approach seventy-five million by the year 2000.

In Cairo, Alexandria, and other urban areas, the exploding population put an enormous strain on the government's ability to provide such basics as housing, water, electricity, and transportation. Cairo's water supply requires massive chlorination, and those who can afford it drink bottled water. Electrical blackouts occur frequently in the section of Cairo known as the "Old City," where about three-fourths of the people live. The streets of Cairo, including the main arteries, become so traffic clogged that it can take several hours to get from one part of the city to another.

Family planning could slow the rate of population growth. But in Egypt there are enormous complications in any attempts at family planning. For one thing, male supremacy is one of the basic social doctrines of Egypt and other Muslim countries. The idea that men are pre-eminent is rooted in the Koran, the sacred book of the

Muslims. Not long ago, Al Azgar University in Cairo, the world's leading Islamic university, published an interpretation of the Koran that stated the "right of protecting and managing the affairs of women is derived from the fact that man is superior to woman by nature...and more powerful and cabable of confirming the struggle of life than women."

Sadat has sought to improve the status of women in marriage and family life through new laws. Although these laws might be considered quite moderate in Western terms, Egyptians look upon them as revolutionary.

Polygamy, the practice of a man having several wives at the same time, is a deep-rooted tradition. If a husband decides to take a second wife, his first wife has no choice but to accept the situation. That tradition has not

By November, 1979, Egypt had regained over half the Sinai. Here Sadat officiates at a flag-raising at Al Arish in honor of the city's return to Egyptian control.

(PRESS & INFORMATION BUREAU, EMBASSY OF THE ARAB REPUBLIC OF EGYPT)

changed. However, this first wife is now permitted to sue for divorce if she disapproves of the second wife.

Another provision of the law concerns the husband's age-old right to disown his wife, ending the marriage by himself. The husband is now required to inform his wife of the divorce. What previously happened was that the husband would not tell the wife he was repudiating her. As a result, she would continue to live with him, producing children whom the man later refused to support.

Still another provision of the new laws has proven controversial, particularly in overcrowded Cairo. This mandates that following a divorce the family apartment is to be awarded to the former wife. "Men came to me and protested most vigorously," Jihan Sadat once told *The New York Times*. "My answer to them was, '*You* can sleep anywhere, but not your wife and children.'"

But many customs have not changed, nor is there any hope that they will in the foreseeable future. In rural areas, for example, children work, helping out in raising crops and tending farm animals. The more children a family has, the higher its income. Another complication common to rural areas concerns the way men think. They believe the more children one has, the more of a man one appears to be.

Many peasant women look upon children as security, especially if the children are boys. The children are the wife's insurance against the day her husband might want to get rid of her. Azziza Hussein, one of the founders of the Egyptian Family Planning Association, has described the problem in these terms. "The woman thinks, 'I'm old, my husband might divorce me, he might spend money elsewhere,' so she continues to have babies."

The mushrooming population growth in rural areas has led to a vast migration to the urban centers. The expansion of cities and towns to accommodate the migrants has required the taking of about a million acres of land in the past thirty years. As a result, there is less land available for farming today than there was in 1950—and the population has more than doubled.

The massive Aswan High Dam, a building project that rivaled the Great Pyramids in size and that began operating in 1968, has proven something of a mixed blessing. While it has served to more than double the country's output of electricity, it has worsened some agricultural problems. By raising the water table, it has permitted salt water to push into the Nile Delta from the Mediterranean Sea. The salt in the water has spoiled crops in many areas.

In addition, the Nile's silt, which used to enrich the Delta soil, is now trapped behind the dam. Farmers must buy fertilizer to provide the soil nutrients that nature once furnished free.

Because of the limited amount of farmable land, Egypt must import as much as 80 percent of its food. Prices for such staples as bread and cooking oil would be exceedingly high were it not for government subsidies, which, in 1980, amounted to more than $2 billion. When Sadat sought to abolish the subsidies in 1977 and prices shot skyward, rioting in the streets was the immediate result. Sadat quickly revoked his order.

The subsidies have not protected the public from the high cost of other items such as meat. Few ordinary people can afford to buy meat. Nor have the subsidies insulated the public from inflation, computed at a rate of about 25 percent in 1980, about double that of the United States for the same year.

During 1980, Sadat sometimes spoke of a "Carter Plan" for Egypt. Similar to the Marshall Plan that helped to rehabilitate Western Europe after World War II, the Carter Plan was to have used many billions of American dollars to trigger economic development in Egypt.

Sadat doesn't talk about the Carter Plan anymore, of course. Carter's defeat in the 1980 election was a jolt to Sadat. He looked forward to meeting with President Ronald Reagan the following year, with hope of establishing a working relationship similar to the one he enjoyed with Carter. But Sadat was enough of a realist to know that any "Reagan Plan," meant to pump American dollars into the Egyptian economy, was out of the question.

A formal portrait of Sadat in his Supreme Commander's uniform.

(PRESS & INFORMATION BUREAU, EMBASSY OF THE ARAB REPUBLIC OF EGYPT)

While Egypt must continue to depend on foreign economic assistance, there are several favorable aspects to the economy. Oil is one. Egypt produces enough oil to fill its own needs and provide a healthy surplus. In 1981 Sadat expected to receive $1 billion from the sale of Eygpt's oil. The country also boasts large, untapped deposits of phosphates and iron ore.

The Suez Canal is another bright spot. The Canal produced $600 million in tolls in 1980. The amount was expected to reach $1 billion in 1981. Egypt also relies on its glittering past for income; that is, from the tourist dollars attracted by the Pyramids and temples.

Sadat has begun to reduce the armed forces. Some money once earmarked for military spending, which at one time accounted for 28 percent of the Egyptian national budget, now goes to development projects or to other national needs.

Sadat sometimes has visitors to Egypt conducted through the still rubble-strewn towns that suffered the severest damage during the Six-Day War of 1967 and the October War of 1973. Since 1967, he tells such groups, hostilities have cost Egypt some $25 billion. "Think what a paradise Egypt would be," he says, "if that had been invested to develop the country."

With a decade or two of peace, Egypt has a chance to become a stable, even a prosperous nation. There are hopeful signs that such stability is beginning to take hold. Entire cities are being planned on the outskirts of Cairo and Alexandria that are to contain new industries. The Egyptian ministries of agriculture and irrigation have announced programs for reclaiming vast stretches of desert terrain that could increase the amount of Egypt's farmable land by three million acres. Plans are being completed for a drainage system that will draw off the excess water of the Nile, the water that causes salt water pollution. Development projects are being planned that will substitute electric power for the water buffalo and other such beasts.

"We have water. We have land," Sadat told Joseph Kraft of *The New Yorker* not long ago. "We have power from the High Dam. We have a good climate and a central location. We have an abundance of skilled labor. All we lack is technology and investment. What we need to do is bring technology and investment from Europe and America. But to do that we must have stability. Stability means, first of all, peace. That is why peace opens the road to prosperity."

The political landscape of the Middle East is vastly different today from what it was in 1970, the year that Sadat became president of Egypt. The years of turmoil are not over. Iraq invaded Iran in 1980. Civil strife engulfed Syria the same year. Libya's Muammar al-Qaddafi continued to promote subversion and terrorism

During the early 1980s, Sadat sought to devote his energies to Egypt's social and economic policies.

whenever the whim struck and in 1981 sent Libyan forces into Chad. The Soviet Union has invaded Afghanistan and established its presence in southern Yemen and Ethiopia.

As the decade of the 1980s began, the Arab–Israeli struggle was stalemated. A final solution was not in sight; yet the danger of war was slight. And for that the world is in debt to Anwar el-Sadat and his vision of peace.

Sadat is permitting himself one monument to that vision. Deep in the Sinai Desert, in Wadi el Raha, the Valley of Rest, at the foot of what is believed to be Mt. Sinai of biblical times, Sadat is building a memorial to peace.

Nearby, Greek Orthodox monks have prayed and studied in the Monastery of St. Catherine for fifteen hundred years. Muhammad gave the monks a written guarantee of safety that is still in their possession.

The area, of course, is also holy to the Jews. It is where they wandered after their flight from Egypt, and where Moses received the stone tablets bearing the Ten Commandments.

The memorial will take the form of three buildings—a church, mosque, and synogogue. Built on a massive scale, the structure is meant to blend in with the rugged mountain landscape.

Sadat has said he wants to be buried at this spot when he dies. But it is not a tomb. "It will be a living symbol of the brotherhood of man," Sadat said, when he announced the project, "a lighthouse that will rekindle the spirit of coexistence and tolerance among nations."

Sadat knows the memorial will not produce world peace. But it is a beacon, a symbol for all, that the vision of Sadat might one day be realized.

INDEX